# SCHOOLING DESIRE

Ursula A. Kelly

SCHOOLING DESIRE

Literacy, Cultural Politics, and Pedagogy

Routledge   New York and London

Published in 1997 by
Routledge
29 West 35th Street
New York, NY 10001

Published in Great Britain by
Routledge
11 New Fetter Lane
London EC4P 4EE

Library of Congress Cataloging-in-Publication Data

Kelly, Ursula Anne Margaret, 1956–
Schooling Desire: literacy, cultural politics, and pedagogy /
Ursula A. Kelly.
p. cm.
Includes bibliographical references and index.
ISBN 0-415-91548-1 (hardcover: alk. paper)
ISBN 0-415-91549-X (pbk: alk. paper)
1. Critical pedagogy. 2. Literacy—Social aspects.
3. Postmodernism and education. I. Title.
LC196.K45   1997
370.11'5—dc20   96-50349
                                 CIP

■ Contents

■ Acknowledgments

■ This book was written in a small fishing community on the Canadian coastline of the Atlantic Ocean where the ordinary and daily and the profound and powerful coexist beautifully. I am thankful for the gift of this place where, sometimes, in a quiet gasp of a moment, desire appears quiet, tender, and free.

Litsa Tsouluhas read the entire manuscript with an intellectual energy and insight both rare and beautiful. I thank her for the invaluable input, given always with care and warm humor.

Pat Singer provided much in a short time: an interest in my work; a watchful, caring eye; and an affirming, gentle, supportive presence. I thank her for removing hurdles when climbing felt impossible.

I thank Ann Wetmore for wise counsel during the last weeks of this project and for helping me convert blurred lines to sharper focus.

My family is an ongoing source of support and love. In this, as in all my work, they warrant my thanks. In particular, I thank my mother, whose integrity, caring, and compassion inspire me always.

I acknowledge the Office of Research at Mount Saint Vincent University for its gesture of support in the final stage of this project.

I thank Jayne Fargnoli, former editor at Routledge, for her interest in and enthusiasm for this project.

Finally, I acknowledge my constant canine companion, the beautiful golden retriever Julie, whose eyes harbor all my hopes and dreams.

SCHOOLING DESIRE

Literacy, Cultural Politics, and Pedagogy

■ The cold, disinfected ambience of stark spaces, muted colors and stale smells, hallmarks of most educational institutions—the "an-aes-thetics" of schools (Pagano 1990, 78–9)—belies the invasive intimacy of the project of schooling. Thronged corridors and classrooms, palpable threats, should more readily remind us that the territory of education is the body, and education territorializes the body. The notion of *mind/ing bodies* bespeaks most accurately and succinctly how the intersection of knowledge, power, and desire craft identity as the cultural project of schools. Schooling, then, is "a mode of social control" (McLaren 1994, 173), a means by which to produce particular forms of subjectivity and to elicit particular forms of participation in social life. These controls are effected through the management and domestication of desire. The sediment of this project of disciplining desire is visible in our most pro-nounced and most (seemingly) innocuous practices; this book mines these workings of desire, tracing their textures, effects, and interests.

The focus on desire in all its forms—discursive, material, and psychoanalytic—is not an attempt to reduce the complex practices of schooling to the workings of desire. Nor is it an effort to domesticate further, by naming more fully the workings of desire, although, in some ways, this effect is unavoidable. As well, I want to distance myself from any sense of "positing desire as the source of a new essentialism" (McRobbie 1994, 67). But, in locating desire as the shape our dreams and identities take in the social, it becomes possible to speculate how it is that desire can work against *and in* our best interests. While schools often mark desire as acceptable or deviant, my concern is with how any utopian inclinations of desire, on any and all cultural sites, might forward emancipatory practices. In this sense, I am as concerned "to make pleasure a serious political question" (Gallop 1988, 104)—along with its attendants, guilt, anxiety, and shame—as I am to insist on and celebrate particular political pleasures.

Schooling Desire arose out of an interest to reflect, from a pedagogical perspective, on developments in critical theories of knowledge, culture, identity, and power and their implications for understanding and transforming practices. The overall purpose of the book, then, is to reiterate and to heighten a sense of the stakes in schooling. Written at a juncture of the theoretical, pedagogical, and autobiographical, the book offers ruminations on the contextual density of schooling and the textual density of culture. In this sense, and in a broad manner, the book is concerned with forms of signification; however, the particular concerns of a broadly conceived literacy education—language, representation, culture, and meaning—are its specific focus. In short, the book addresses and attempts to articulate how the challenges of a postmodern culture require a vastly different notion of literacy than the dominant notions that circulate within education. I argue throughout this book that literacy education needs to be reconceptualized within the postmodern as part of an educational project inspired by the diverse and divergent, but best, inclinations of poststructural theories, critical literacies, cultural studies, and radical pedagogies.

More specifically, *Schooling Desire* draws on critical theories of literacy, culture, and pedagogy and utilizes various textual forms to frame and illustrate the relationship of the culture of pedagogy and the pedagogy of culture (Grossberg 1994) to the construction, deployment, and regulation, through schooling, of desire. Its objectives are to critique traditional and dominant notions of literacy education and schooling, to reconceptualize these notions using the lenses of feminist, poststructural, and cultural theories, and, in so doing, to position the workings of desire at the heart of a transformative pedagogy while critiquing both socially regressive and progressive structurings of fulfillment, pleasure, and desire. Examples from biography and pedagogy, and from popular sources such as film, advertisements, and photography, provide the means by which to analyze the pedagogical dilemmas posed by many current practices within contemporary schooling. Through these practices—writing autobiography, reading popular culture, educating across difference—particular practices of desire are silenced and enunciated (that is, *schooled*) and specific social identities are constituted and negotiated.

Schooling Desire is divided into seven chapters. While each chapter, in many ways, exists as a discrete essay, the arguments of each chapter are informed by those of the preceding one(s), all of which culminate in an overall argument for a particular project and for a broad-based pedagogy of desire. The chapters focus several major themes in a post-structural critical literacy: language/discourse; biography; culture; difference; and desire. Written from various, multiple, and even contradictory positions, these chapters are haunted by the moody, broody postmodern subject. The following synopses indicate the scope of each chapter and demonstrate how each contributes to the overall focus of the book.

In the first chapter, the theoretical premises of *Schooling Desire* are established through an extensive outline and critique of both the discourses informing present conceptualizations of schooling, curriculum, literacy, language, culture, and pedagogy, and the structurings of desire they mobilize. Psychoanalytic, material, and discursive notions of desire are articulated as the informing basis of the discussions to follow. The culminating argument is for a disruption of dominant notions of literacy and a broadened reconceptualization of literacies as technologies of cultural embodiment, social practice, and regulated desire. To address adequately the political dimensions of these technologies, and our dialectical relation to theme as subjects, I argue for a radical pedagogy of desire, based in poststructural insights. The beginning place for such a pedagogy are the already embodied and presently circulating social practices of literacies of the popular, the cultural, and the experiential.

Chapter 2 establishes the philosophical and pedagogical bases of an emphasis on language as the cornerstone of a pedagogy of desire. Working from the psychoanalytic insight that desire is forever displaced, "on the one hand culturally promoted, and on the other linguistically blocked" (Silverman 1983, 77), I attempt to trace the significance for literacy of "the repression that is the tax exacted by the use of language" (Wright 1984, 109). Also examined are the social and political implications for pedagogy of the argument that "[t]here is an incessant struggle within language, because it is at once cause and effect of the body's desire" (Wright 1984, 176). With its focus on discourse, text, and subjectivity, and our often conflicted and contradictory relationship to, and embodiment of, language and realities, poststructural theory can provide useful analytic tools by which to discern the complexities of language and the incarnation of desire. However, as I note in Chapter 2, turning poststructural theory on the self can be as distressing as it can be hopeful. Radical pedagogies informed by the theoretical insights of poststructural theory and attentive to the colonizing imperatives of theories are presented as a mechanism for hopeful change within projects of renegotiating desire.

The third chapter provides a focus on the ways in which auto/biography offers one place from which to address how literacy and the contexts and practices of culture are intertwined in readings of our selves, our histories, and our social places, that is, in the production of forms of subjectivity. *French Lessons*, a memoir by Alice Kaplan, forms the basis of a beginning discussion of desire, identity, pedagogy, and culture. In this chapter, I argue that, as readings of our lives through the present, auto/biography both reveals *and* conceals and is a site on which desire is announced to be at once depleted and deferred. If, as Nicole Brossard (1990) claims, "reality is confinement, a little grave that misleads desire" (169), then auto/biography may be seen as the grave's monument. Auto/biographies, as always-ever partial versions of reality, are tales of literacy and, as such, are educational stories: telltale signs of the negotiation and maneuvering of competing forms of subjectivity, meanings and desire on offer in and through the literacies of culture, including the culture of schooling. These points are demonstrated through an analysis of a photo-accompanied autobiography, part of a class exercise in examining the interrelationship of power, desire, and subjectivity.

Chapter 4 focuses on popular culture and provides an argument for the need to approach engagements with and readings of popular culture as practices of literacy. The discourses that surround and that are produced through popular culture, as forms of knowledge, inform identity, and, therefore, warrant critical attention. As incessantly circulating commentaries on and of the social, popular culture is ignored to our educational disadvantage, for it is in the success of the popular that the structuring of desire is most evidenced. Giroux and Simon (1989) argue convincingly for "a pedagogy of pleasure and meaning" (1) grounded in the popular and in students' experiences of and relation to the popular.

The purpose of this chapter is to explore the dimensions of a pedagogy that begins with the popular and the patterns of desire that inform and are formed through popular culture. Using the insights of cultural studies, which provide the means to access the constraints and possibilities of cultural practices, an argument is made for the role of pedagogy and cultural studies—cultural pedagogies—in engaging and furthering literacies of the popular.

In Chapter 5, I develop a notion of disarming femininities which I argue are a production of manipulations of desire ignored, denied, or inadequately addressed in schools. Using a reading of the Atom Egoyan film *Exotica*, I critique the social malfunctions of desire across the lines of difference to demonstrate how cultural forms can simultaneously privilege and contest dominant social relations. In particular, I deconstruct a specific form of subjectivity, that of the schoolgirl, as a means to address issues of gaze, power, and desire. Within the postmodern, contemporary fears and anxieties are heightened against a backdrop of social insurgence, instability, and perceived nihilism. Yet these same fears and anxieties are tracked onto forms of subjectivity through the structuring of desire as discourses of violence and decay and threat to our psychic and social realities. In the face of such technologies of desire, the perpetual failure by schools to address their institutional implication in the problem indicates a more insidious educational crisis than that to which conservative critics point. This crisis accentuates the need for a response built upon a project of enablement, agency, and resistance.

Chapter 6 focuses on the formulation of a project of and about difference through which utopian, revolutionary longings may be articulated into a far-reaching denial of dominance and a simultaneous celebration of difference. Drawing on postcolonial theories, I explore here how desire is implicated in both constructions and distortions of difference. The chapter addresses how a pedagogy of and for difference might promote cultural growth and sustenance through recognizing the cultural and political dimensions of literacy, difference, and identity and by addressing the disabling contradictions, for the Other, of practicing literacy on the terms and the terrain of the dominant—literacy as an affront to difference. At the heart of an enabling project of difference, I suggest, is the exploration of how desire is represented, regulated, and transformed in the name of literacy as the practice of making identities.

The final chapter uses a personal engagement with the film *To Sir with Love* to address the eros of pedagogy. At its most frightening, a pedagogical project of desire has the potential to be understood as the appropriation of the stories and cultures of those deemed Other (Giroux and Simon 1989, 25), as the bourgeois intellectualization of desire (Walkerdine 1990, 201), or as a project of malignant social assimilation of the sort informed by the rampant exploitations of global difference. At its most hopeful, however, such a project demands the unrelenting acknowledgement of the structuring of desire as an implicit part of all pedagogies. In this latter sense, as Roger Simon (1992) insists, "the erotic character of a pedagogy of possibility" can, and I would argue must, be founded on "a fascination with the dignity and worth of those whom we teach" (72). The purpose of the final chapter, then, is twofold: to articulate the link of eros and pedagogy; to locate eros within personal and political investments in pedagogy; and to explore the ways in which radical pedagogies might be informed and forewarned by a renewed claim on the eros of teaching.

This book was conceived through and driven by the desire to restore the focus of teaching to its designated workplace, the site of construction—the subject-body, the embodied subject. Through its writing, I came to understand better and to reconfigure my own educational desires, the designs that inhabit my own teaching/body. If "the proper measure of learning is personal" (Gallop 1995, 79), as I have implied throughout this book, then the intimate contours of the experiences of learning might be said to shore up the long arm of desire.

Schooling Desire poses as an academic exercise. Thinking through theory—that is, mapping one's life onto discursive forms that authorize ways of speaking about experiences—exerts more than a measure of control over those experiences. In a way that this book attempts to demonstrate, such discursive mapping is an effect of, as it also elicits, desires. This haunting sense of a subject searching for the unattainable discursive position from which the pain of desire, the seemingly unyielding urge for wholeness, might be eased abates as this project finds closure.

If to study the constitutive base of desire is, ultimately, part of a project to "consolidate oneself as a subject of lack" (Silverman 1996, 37), then this goal is a worthwhile and hopeful one for the subjects of radical pedagogies. This mammoth task requires that the literacy project at the heart of modernist schooling be fundamentally revamped. The reach of desire into discourse might, then, be more tender, its bodily contours more gentle, and its social consequences less devastating.

One

RE/CONCEPTUALIZATIONS

*Literacy, Desire,
and Pedagogy*

■ The discussions that unfold in the following chapters are informed by a series of theoretical assumptions about literacy, culture, and pedagogy. In particular, these discussions attempt to galvanize issues of desire in practices of literacy, culture and pedagogy. As such, the specific conceptualizations offered here locate these literacy practices as designs of and on desires, dreams, and longings as they relate to forms of participation in social visioning and transformation. This focus is not meant to reduce the complex workings of the multiple dimensions of the practices of literacy, culture, and pedagogy; rather, working with such multifaceted complexities shores up the centrality of desire within radical pedagogies of literacy and culture. This chapter traces these interdices: the intricacies of desire with/in social dreams of difference—affective investments in social change.

■ Toward Literacies

Despite the common reference to literacy in the singular, where the unspoken or unstated adjective is most often "functional," as in functional literacy, there is both a theoretical and a practical need to insist on the plural—literacies. Literacy—the practices of literacy—and being literate—the embodiment of forms of literacies—are socially, historically, and culturally contingent. As social practice, doing literacy varies according to availability, need, audience, context, etc. As embodiment, literacy practices shape identities, defining as much a consciousness as a set of relationships between conscious communities and specific technologies of literacy. These practices and relationships are diverse and multiple. Thus, literacy falsely suggests a set of practices that are univocal and generic, thereby denying literacies, the myriad ways in which seemingly generic skills are practiced—imported, adopted, adapted, and transformed within specific cultural frameworks. In this sense, literacies cannot be separated from literacies *of* (the technologies of literacy practices), literacies *for* (the social visions that accompany such practices), and, literacies *where* (the social context in which these practices are located: the cultural politics of literacy).

Such specific cultural politics of literacy may be demonstrated through a notation of the often marked distinction between school literacies and popular literacies. School literacies are the practices of (usually) reading and writing associated with prescribed curricular (usually print) texts for teacher-prescribed purposes and pedagogically prescriptive outcomes. Popular literacies are the practices of reading, writing, viewing, etc., that encompass a more intimate relationship of culture and identity, one less obviously and actually regulated by the expectations of formal schooling in literacy education and English Studies. In this comparison, the meanings and values placed on each of these literacies cannot be separated from who practices each, under what circumstances and under whose surveillance, and with what pleasures and effects. Further, the very opposition demarcates a taken-for-granted hierarchy, which, rather than being in any way *natural* is actually actively produced within—and against—these literacies, an insidious enactment of the cultural politics of literacy.

Literacy is also informed by a variety of discourses, i.e., functional literacy, critical literacy, etc., which define the specific *form* of literacy and how the form itself does indeed form and regulate what it means to do literacy and to be literate—that is, the social project of specific literacies. As will be further clarified in forthcoming discussions, there are also differences between forms of literacy. For example, cultural literacy encompasses a much different agenda for students as citizens than does critical literacy. Cultural literacy seeks to create a responsible citizenry who accepts and participates suitably in the present social order. Critical literacy seeks to create a citizenry who questions the inequities of the social order and who can exercise productive agency toward its transformation.

Further, *within* forms of literacy are also competing theoretical positions. Critical literacy, for example, may encompass a variety of perspectives, i.e., Marxist, feminist, and poststructural, etc., each of which would lay claim to a specific direction for critical literacy. As well, the postmodern, with its accompanying implosion, necessitates an articulation of hybrid literacies, ways of producing and representing texts and meaning that encompass an array of literacy technologies, of which print is merely one. Literacy, then, is a complex, shifting, and even misleading signifier. For these very reasons, it is important to present a broader articulation of its complexities as a signifier as they pertain to both social vision and social practice, not to anchor it as a signifier but to heighten the significance of its nuances. An examination of the various *forms* of literacy is a useful place from which to begin such a discussion.

Some theorists have noted that, out of the array of discourses that frame current educational discussions of literacy, three forms predominate: functional literacy, cultural literacy, and critical literacy (Green 1993; Lankshear and McLaren 1993). A more comprehensive picture of informing discourses of literacy is presented by Ball, Kenny, and Gardiner (1990), who identify four, rather than three, forms of literacy: functional, cultural, progressive, and critical. Their picture is more useful, for it explicitly distinguishes progressive literacy from critical literacy, a separation I find more accurate and more politically astute, for such separation denies the unfounded claim to radicalism of progressive literacy. Further, it challenges the hegemony of progressive literacy within an educational context where "soft liberalism" (Portelli 1995, 8) can be and is often mistaken for critical literacy and pedagogy.

The forms of literacy presented by Ball et al. (1990) emerge from a historical tracing of the discourses that inform English teaching, English being that curriculum subject whereon the major articulations of literacy have been framed since its appearance as a school subject but a century ago. As these authors and others (Green 1990, 1993; Hamilton 1993; Morgan 1990, 1993, 1995) note, however, the development of particular forms of literacy was and is never separate from particular forms of morality. That is, literacy was and remains a social and moral project, an inseparable blend of notions of the civil and the literate, a domesticating practice with specific, identifiable interests, those of nation(-making) and state(-controlling). Ball et al. argue that such historic and contemporary coupling of literacy and morality make forms of literacy practice and literacy pedagogy undeniably political, a point reiterated by large numbers of theorists across the spectrum of literacy studies (Gilbert 1991; Luke 1991, 1991a, 1994; Macedo 1993; Patterson 1992). Regarding this point, Allan Luke (1991) insists, "[t]here are no exemptions to offer. Teaching the word, we selectively socialize students into versions of the world, into possible worlds, and into a version of the horizons and limits of literate competence" (139).

In the promotion, practices, and pedagogies of literacies, of utmost concern, then, are the attendant, even if unstated or unintentioned, political, social, and moral visions. Ball, Kenny, and Gardiner (1990) present these literacies and their accompanying social visions, an encapsulation of which follows. *Functional literacy* is a "literacy of skills" (77) driven by workforce needs and marketplace ideologies. Its accompanying curriculum is pre-packaged and restrictive; its pedagogical focus is individualistic, behaviorist, and competitive. *Cultural literacy* is a "literacy of morality" (79) in which, through great literature, a shared sensibility and culture is acquired. Its accompanying curriculum is closed and elitist; its pedagogy is authoritarian, humanist, and universalizing. *Progressive literacy* is a "literacy of personal discovery" (80) at the center of which are ideologies of personal growth, individualism, and expressivism. Its curriculum is open and pluralistic; its pedagogy is student centered and liberalist. *Critical literacy* is a literacy of social transformation in which the ideological foundations of knowledge, culture, schooling, and identity-making are recognized as unavoidably political, marked by vested interests and hidden agendas. Its curriculum is the everyday world as text and the analytic frameworks necessary to deconstruct it; its pedagogy is situated, interrogative, and counter-hegemonic.

My contention—insufficiently highlighted in literacy studies—is that literacy practices manufacture, that is, form, shape, and regulate, human desires. In any of the aforementioned forms and practices of literacy, how desire is manipulated, regulated, and recast as consumer and cultural ethics is easily discerned. The discourses that inform each of these literacies position students and teachers in ways that define—and, therefore, confine—sense and sensibility. If language is constitutive of subjectivity, that is, the meanings we make of ourselves are derived from those available to us in language, and desire is constituted, that is, shaped and spoken, through language (indeed, is an *effect* of language)—concepts more fully developed in Chapter 2—then inextricable links among language, desire, and subjectivity form the political fabric of all literacies. A crucial question becomes, then, how it is that these connections are written into the forms of literacy outlined above.

The construction of desire is always a specific, historical practice, manifested culturally and collectively across a range of differences. This character of desire is demonstrated in historical shifts and changes in what is deemed pleasurable and possible in a given context for specific peoples. No literacy curriculum and/or pedagogy can harness completely and/or be singularly responsible for the determinations of human desire; yet desires, as practices in many ways bound and determined by language, are implicated in the construction of desire. As enacted disciplinary practices—practices that by design and effect regulate, domesticate, and discipline notions of desire—literacy curriculum and pedagogy position student-subjects to read and to write the world in specific ways. As powerful institutionalized practices, forms of literacy compete or complement other discursive practices that position students in relation to the social order as subjects desiring specific forms of human life. In short, we learn to desire some things and not others as ways of participating in and of being literate in the world. For example, the accompanying curricula and pedagogies of functional and cultural literacies position students to define their scope of responsibility and participation as particular kinds of worker-citizens whose capabilities determine their place within an already established, although not fixed, stratified social order. The cultural accoutrements, also stratified, that attend these placements, reiterate this order. Here, culture is object and commodity, a statement of position, place, and possibility, the desirable "drag" necessary for social mobility and social statement.

Together, functional and cultural literacies enlist "pedagogy as domestication" (Lankshear and McLaren 1993, 21) or "pedagogy as adaptation" (Giroux 1994, 158) by actively encouraging the internalization of social hierarchies so that those positioned differentially, unequally, understand such a fate as a consequence of inadequacy—inculturated as incapable. Here, desire is defined, paradoxically, both within and beyond the strictures of possibility, destined to (dis)satisfaction through the available, its excesses projected beyond the available. Those positioned through privilege understand such positioning as the just desserts of capability, hard work, and/or birthright. Here, desire is located in and through the available, its excesses projected beyond the available into the (unattainable) Other, that which is cast aside, despised, or feared, that against which privilege must protect itself.

Progressive literacy, operating in "the heady glow of personalism and child-centerdness" (Gilbert 1991, 204), the naiveté of "I'm okay, you're okay" offers little by way of alternative to the more overt structurings of desire through functional and cultural literacies. As Valerie Walkerdine (1990), in her sustained critique of progressivism, notes, "regulation had gone underground" (36), not disappeared. Lisa Delpit (1988) puts it just as succinctly in her criticisms of progressivist (whole language) practices: "to act as if power does not exist is to ensure that the power status quo remains the same" (292). As these writers and others (Harman and Edelsky 1989) have insisted, such progressivism further alienates those already disenfranchised, for it nurtures individual desires without attention to either the social conditions that delimit them or the means by which to transform these conditions, the practice of social dreaming.

Attention to the latter would be a move toward "reflective desire" (Davies 1993, 169), an objective of a critical literacy. A literacy that positioned students to reflect on the myriad ways in which personal and social desires are shaped and delimited through engagements with cultural meanings would define students as critical agents, more than prisoners, of technologies and their meanings. Through a critical literacy, the regulatory effects of meanings and their intersections with identity and desire—aspects of the cultural politics of all literacy practices— would be central. Such practices of reflective desire would be no less attentive to its own textual dimensions, means by which reflective desire actively structures its own position as desirable. Patti Lather (1991) refers to such deconstructions of discourse-text-desire as a means "to probe the libidinal investment in form and content of the author-text relationship. It is to mark the belief that our discourse is the meaning of our longing" (83).

Critical literacy, then, can be posited as a form of literacy that embraces the development and practices of literacies and, simultaneously, the interrogation of what constitutes such literacies: texts, practices, contexts, not as separate constructs in an overall schema of literacy practice(s) but as mutually but not equally informing relations in the overall (and at any given) social moment of literacy. Critical literacy is vigilant in addressing the relationship of literacies, power, culture and identity, for literacies are seen to inform both "our reading the word and the world" (Freire and Macedo 1987). Such a relationship is never innocent or ever absent; as such, it must (re)direct our questions about literacy practices. As Lankshear and McLaren (1993) note

> If literacies largely inform how we read the world and the word, but also how such a reading produces who we are and how we dream our social present, then we need to explore the changing relationship between literacy and culture. . . . (3–4)

Such a relationship rests not only on a reconceptualization of literacy, but also on a reconceptualization of language and culture.

■ Language and Culture

Central to an account of literacy and cultural politics is an accompanying notion of language that refuses the often taken-for-granted (mis)understanding of language as objective expression of thought and reality, the ideology of language implicit in much of educational practice. An account of language as cultural politics entails a recognition of the various discourses through which language is conceptualized, their associated practices and their implicit and explicit political possibilities and limitations. For the sake of consistency and linearity, I shall reference these discourses in relation to the forms of literacy explicated in the previous section.

Several writers have attempted to categorize the approaches to language theory and broadly based notions of educational practice (Graddol 1994; Christie 1993; Morgan 1987). In presenting categories of language theory or models of language, it is important to note the attendant conceptions of the individual language user and society and culture. As David Graddol (1994) notes

> Models of language are not just built to explain empirical data. Language is so intimately connected with social life and human behavior that any model of language tends to embody assumptions and value judgements which cannot be challenged by empirical data because they already circumscribe what kind of data is regarded as relevant to the theory. In this respect, a model of language can also be said to represent an *ideology* of language. (9)

In his own account, Graddol offers a succinct and insightful presentation of three models of language that highlight such ideological interrelationships. These models—*structural*, *social*, and *postmodern*—provide a useful context from which to argue for an explicit study of language as cultural politics.

The first model of language presented by Graddol, the structural model, is a descriptive one. The primary focus of the structural model of language is "the material substance of language" (1), through which a form of "methodical analysis" may be applied, reaping regulatory language management strategies from communication itself. As Graddol notes, such description is made possible through the reduction of communication to direct transmission and precise correspondents, the isolation of language from its variable sociocultural contexts, and a focus on so-called ideal language use. Within this model, language has an essential syntax, the machinations of which reveal the workings of language and of the human mind. This model of language is, in part, what Frances Christie (1993) calls "a received tradition of English teaching" (76), the artificial separation of the study of language, largely through systems of grammar, from meaning. This model of language informs both *functional* and *cultural* literacies each with its emphasis on the restrictive decoding of texts.

Graddol's second model, the social model, is a contextual one. The primary focus of the social model is the interrelationship of language, culture, and identity, the argument being that "linguistic structure alone cannot determine meaning" (2). As Graddol notes, a social model of language does not abandon structural principles of language; rather, it relates them to societal structures, bringing a greater correspondence of factors to bear on language usage. The social model of language romanticizes the individual, culture, and language usage and encourages diversity of language use as the maintenance of individually and culturally unique expression of/and meaning. This model of language, while attendant to the social, inadequately addresses the full implications of language as a social medium, one that constructs reality as well as one out of which reality is constructed. This model of language displays the same liberal pluralism that informs *progressive* literacy. Ironically, though, this model of language was never extensively applied within progressive literacy practices, many of which focused on meaning-making and less on the restrictive nature of the very medium to which meaning is enslaved (Christie 1993).

The third model proposed by Graddol, the postmodern (for Graddol, synonymous with poststructural), is an iconoclastic one. The primary focus of the postmodern model is the practice of signifying conceived as "a broader semiotic view of what language consists of" (17) beyond the confines of structure and coherence. As Graddol notes, the postmodern model "represents an attempt to understand the fragmentary flux of language not by idealising simple underlying mechanisms but by attempting to tease apart and understand the nature of the fragmentation" (2). The postmodern model of language disrupts the notion of the rational, unified, and individualistic language user/meaning-maker and the stability of meaning and replaces them with a never fully knowing subject who is pre-spoken, in contradictory ways, by broadly based language systems that constitute the subject in multiple, imprecise, and conflicting ways. This model of language has a political usefulness, for it positions subjects in a reflective stance toward language as constitutive and constituting. In other words, this model of language provides the means by which to articulate the relationship of language, culture, and identity as "dialogic" (Morgan 1987, 453) rather than linear, coherent, and fixed. It is the enhancement of this reflective stance, as a means to advance political struggle, to which many adherents of *critical* literacy have consigned their work.

Within each of these models, issues of desire are delimited in particular ways. In the structural model of language, desire and language are related only in that language is a tool of expression, the site on which an essentialized desire is spoken. Here, desire is regulated and bound in the name of a stable order. In the social model of language, desire is idiosyncratic and culturally bound, an expression of individual meaning-making within a determinate context. In the postmodern model of language, desire is erratic and "sought, bought and packaged" (Coward 1985) in the interests of particular constituencies at particular historical moments. In this model, desire is an effect of language, only partially informed by and constituted in consciousness and language. This relationship of desire and language, as articulated in this model of language—and more fully explained in Chapter 2—captures the embodied effects of language, that is, the body as a constellation of language, desire, power, and identity.

Of the three models of language presented by Graddol, the postmodern/poststructural model reaps the greatest insights into the complex interrelations of language, culture, desire, power, and subjectivity, my concerns in this work. While often considered anarchic (the death of meaning) and non-agenic (the impossibility of subjects exercising agency in the constituting of their own realities), this model of language centers language (and language-related systems) in social meaning, revealing its regulatory work and, in so doing, posing the huge but not impossible task of creating possibility for a world of difference.

■ **Culture With/In the Postmodern**[1]

Renewed and institutionally powerful cries for "cultural literacy" have accompanied nearly two decades of a resurgence of conservative politics in Western democracies. For advocates of cultural literacy, culture includes the *rituals*, *traditions*, and *objects* selected by a dominant group as representative of its lifestyle, struggles, and victories. Culture, here, is not only selective but elitist, not only closed but also often openly hostile to unassimilable Others for, ultimately, culture here is a history of a particular notion of civilization spawned in the Enlightenment, fueled in schooling through Arnoldian and Leavisite English,[2] the legacies of which much of the curriculum subject of English still enshrines, and reclaimed in this usage. Herein, culture also carries another legacy of the Enlightenment: "to enlighten some was to regulate many others" (McRobbie 1994, 8). It is to employ excessive understatement to claim that, within an undeniably postcolonial and postmodern age, an age also enriched by a long history of feminist insights, it is no longer educationally feasible or morally reasonable to insist on such singularity of culture.

A more useful definition of culture points to *processes* and *practices* by which the social relations that position a group—through social categories and/or constellations—are defined, contested, legitimized, and transformed. Within this notion of culture is its acknowledgement of the intimate relationship of culture and subjectivity and the presence of power as an indissoluble character of all cultural practices. As processes and practices constitutive of subjectivity, culture might be most effectively approached as an amalgam of partial and contingent "identity-articulations" (Morgan 1993, 111)—embodied meanings negotiated within a vast field of cultural hypertextuality. Such a definition marks a shift of emphasis from object to process: culture as identity-formation and relational social practice.

The interrelationship of culture, power, and identity is the focus of research in cultural studies (see Chapter 4). Cultural studies focuses the complexity of culture by the

> examining of all those processes which accompany the production of meaning in culture, not just the end-product: from where it is socially constructed to where it is socially deconstructed and contested, in the institutions, practices and relationships of everyday life around us. (McRobbie 1994, 41)

Within such research, the thorny issue of desire is repeatedly identified as the tie that binds meanings of self to/and culture. The phenomenon of "cloistered literacies" (Luke 1994, 372)—common practices defined around popular genre/form and designate community, for example, young girls reading romance novels (Christian-Smith 1990, 1993; Willinsky and Hunniford 1993; Gilbert and Taylor 1991)—well demonstrate these connections. Such connections are not confined to print forms. Researchers have pointed to the complexities of audience "reading" practices around film (Walkerdine 1990), music, i.e., hip-hop (Dyson 1993; Walcott 1995), fashion (McRobbie 1994), and architecture (Morris 1993). As interactive text, culture can be read from, read as, and read against; as social texts, such interactions are delimited and delimiting. In the uptake can be seen the sites of intervention, accommodation, and reconstitution, the pedagogical inclinations of subjectivity-in-culture, culture-in-subjectivity.

Such research has profound implications for literacy and literacy pedagogy. If culture is *pedagogical*, that is, if culture shapes our relationship to knowledge and our understandings of ourselves—to which research in cultural studies attests, a point not lost on critical educators[3] (Giroux 1994; Giroux and Simon 1989; Grossberg 1994)—then critical literacy becomes instrumental in identifying how such shaping occurs, the processes by which culture works to inform readings of the world. What is also clear from such understandings of the pedagogy of culture is the extent to which there is also a culture of pedagogy (Grossberg 1994), curriculum, and schooling in the sense that each of these are definitional of social relations of knowing, being, and possibility. Cultural studies, thus, allows the realization of aspects of education as cultural practices through which meanings are produced, circulated, and engaged. The very politics of such cultural processes and practices is the site of the intersection of cultural studies and critical education.

Whereas cultural studies has redefined and expanded the traditional educational domain of literacy (Giroux 1994) and the cultural domain of education, simultaneously, postmodern times announce the conditions of other "emergent literacies" (Spencer 1986). Despite anachronistic insistences on print-centrism by many educators, postmodern culture (see Chapter 4) surpasses any single technology of meaning. Within the postmodern, cultural forms are often characterized by implosion, hybridity, and multi-mediation. The challenge of literacy education within the postmodern is to address itself to these broad cultural changes in ways that encourage critical interrogation rather than refusal or denial, that seek libratory and transformative inclinations rather than presume negativity and passivity, and that center multiplicity and diversity rather than monolithism and homogenization. In other words, literacy within the postmodern must move beyond its modernist tendencies to embrace new subjectivities and new practices emerging through vastly expanding communications technologies.

■ Curriculum as Cultural Politics

Traditional notions of curriculum are encased in modernist ideals of authoritative and objective knowledge, rationality, and scientism. Such curriculum presents "grand narratives" of history, civilization, and progress as cultural objects of consumption, the necessary accoutrements of an educated citizen of a modern nation. Within such curriculum, transcendental signifiers—Democracy, Truth, Reason, etc.—operate to organize, to contain, and to stabilize meaning in the interests of the modern nation state. The authority of such curriculum is, itself, secured by such signifiers, which are surrounded by textual canonical props selected to delimit contestation. Such curriculum positions students to develop what is believed to be their innate capacity for reason within the disciplinary structures provided by curriculum and its attendant transmission and behaviorist-based pedagogies. Curriculum, herein constituted as object, is revised on the basis of "new knowledge" accrued through the progressive evolution of human understanding of the objective laws of "man and nature."

For my purposes here, a counter-notion of curriculum is necessary, one that challenges dominant assertions of curriculum. This counter-notion is posited poststructurally and critically as "a discourse and an organized structure of social relations [that] has represented both an expression and an enforcer of particular relations of power" (Giroux 1990, 3); in other words, as a form of cultural politics. In this sense, curriculum is always quite active: a poststructural series of readings (Lather 1991, 145) or rewritings circulated through formal networks of schooling and pedagogy. Through the institutional base of schools, curriculum serves as the planned means by which some discourses are legitimized and others marginalized or silenced. Such curriculum positions teachers and students in particular (and regulatory) ways in relation to specified forms of knowledge, through both their absence and presence, and to specific notions of knowledge-production. As such, curriculum is itself a process and practice active in the production of subjectivities, of knowing subjects—schooled subjects—whose engagement with curriculum is relational, that is, based on relations of power into which subjects are (re)positioned differently and inequitably.

Cast as cultural politics, curriculum presents itself as a project for critical literacy, as the very object of study to which students may direct at least some of their questions of schooling practices. As Colin Lankshear (1993) insists, there is a need to "ask serious questions about what curriculum should be aiming *to make literacy into*" (156). Lankshear's question is double-edged: How are already existing "extracurricular," i.e., popular, literacies (see Chapter 4) reconfigured, that is, contained and managed by curriculum, and how might school literacies—what curriculum has traditionally *made of* literacy—be more effectively transformed by the project of critical literacy itself? Herein lie the challenges for educators to not only acknowledge the postmodern condition but to position ourselves and our students critically within the array of signifying practices that characterize the postmodern as subject-agents seeking pleasure *and* transformation. The tools of poststructuralism provide an important entry point into such a project.

■ Poststructural Literacies

The varied threads of the preceding discussions may be summarized in an argument for what I would call a poststructural literacy. The advantages of such terminology lie in its enactment of a *mode of analysis* or *theoretical practice* that centers discourse, representation, subject (reader) positions, and cultural practices as the focal lenses for the hypertextuality of postmodern life—the means to a critical practice with/in the postmodern. Such a mode of analysis shifts attention from individualism to subjectivity, from text to discursive practices, and from signifier to signifying practices. Its focus is on how language works, in whose and what interests, on what cultural sites, and why. A poststructural literacy is a theoretical and methodological means by which to create a critical literacy; in other words, it is a critical literacy forged out of the insights of poststructural theories. Figure 1 provides a brief summary of the modern/postmodern and structural/poststructural divide, suggesting their similarities and differences through literacies, curriculum, pedagogies, etc.

Poststructural theories have been used to forward many standpoints within a politics of difference: queer, feminist, and postcolonial. As such it has demonstrated its political usefulness across a range of difference. What it provides is not the funeral bed for the death of the subject, as some have argued, but the usurping of the tyranny of the unified subject; what it denies is not the agency of the subject but the continued romanticization of the overstated productive capacities of the modernist, humanist subject. As such, it is attuned to the "terrible beauties" of human struggle, the impossible underbelly of possibility. Such is not nihilism but, rather, refusal to *underwrite* the complexities of systems of meaning. The cautionary tales of many theorists (Ebert 1991; Giroux 1994; Jay 1995; Lankshear and McLaren 1993) underscore the dangers of poststructural theories but do not eliminate the importance of poststructural insights to a transformative project within the postmodern.

Of the range of analytic tools available, at present, a poststructural literacy offers one effective means of addressing "the coercive character of texts to shape desire, to constitute 'real selves' that are positioned in 'real worlds' (Davies 1993, 148). Texts, here, must be understood beyond the parameters of Davies's reference and the rigid borders of containment that held texts as entities; instead, texts are fluid constructs, the permeable boundaries of which are continually negotiated in the intersection of knowledge, power, culture, and desire. Similarly, notions of selfhood are undone, too, losing their immutability in a trade-off of essence for construction, stability for contradiction, and destiny for agency. Davies (1993) takes note of this shift, too:

> The stranglehold of humanist and enlightenment discourses on the nature of personhood necessarily loosen their grip once they are seen as discursive constructions rather than the transparent forms of words they claimed to be, forms of words which make possible, we were persuaded to believe, descriptions of "real selves." The *innocence* of language as a transparent medium for describing the real world is undone in poststructuralist theory, revealing a rich mosaic of meaning and structure through which we speak ourselves and are spoken into existence. (148)

Once the innocence of language is undone, the space is created for an articulation of the political nature of text and meaning, and of identity constituted within textual meaning *cum* knowledge-making. Therein, too, lies the political dimensions of culture, for it is within the textuality of culture that identity and meaning are (re)constituted. And as Allan Luke (1991) notes here and reiterates elsewhere (Luke 1993),

> in the text saturated environment where texts are commodities and commodities themselves have become powerful signifiers, students also need languages of criticism and scrutiny. Prerequisite is the introduction of the teaching of discourse critique and critical reading positions, even in early childhood. (142)

■ **Locating Desire**

Some of the most provocative work addressing the construction of desire and subjectivity through culture and schooling is that of feminist scholars working with the problematics of women's and young girls' desires (Christian-Smith 1990; Cherland and Edelsky 1993; Gilbert and Taylor 1991; Moss 1989; Willinsky and Hunniford 1986). This problem is captured by Rosalind Coward (1985) in one of the earliest and most accessible studies of female desire:

> Feminine [subject] positions are produced as responses to the pleasures offered us; our subjectivity and identity are formed in the definitions of desire which encircle us. These are the experiences which make change such a difficult and daunting task, for female desire is constantly lured by discourses which sustain male privilege. (16)

Such insights impel unwavering scrutiny of the complex workings of desire, for it is here, in the realm of pleasure and longing, that change meets its greatest obstacle—hegemonic desire.

Much of the current research on desire points to its many dimensions. For example, Christian-Smith (1993, 3–4) argues that desire has at least three dimensions: psychological, discursive, and material. As Christian-Smith employs these terms, the *psychological*—what I would more aptly term the psychoanalytic—refers to the place of the unconscious in desire. In this psychoanalytic dimension, desire arises as longings accrued from now split and suppressed aspects of what were once fuller, more unified selves to which desire beckons a return, a closing of the gap which is dissatisfaction and fissure, and out of which desire arises. It is through the *discursive*, through (regulatory) language practices, that desire is shaped and constituted—desire's reach into discourse. Insofar as these discourses of desire—the language practices through which desire is named, constituted, spoken—point us to commodity consumption as the site of desire's fulfillment, desire has a *material* dimension.

In that the latter two dimensions of desire—discursive and material—are disciplinary and work to shape, regulate, and domesticate desire, it can be said that desire has a fourth, *schooled*, dimension. Naming this dimension brings questions of the disciplinary logic of the discursive practices utilized by a broad range of cultural institutions more explicitly to the fore. Through such practices, desire is enlisted to meet particular social ends through the promise of pleasure in exchange for the participation of the desiring subject in this logic. Desire finds its expression in the social; but desire is also bound by the social. For the desiring subject, this connection secures "discourse as the meaning of our longing" (Lather 1991, 83), the constitutive site of desire, meaning, positionality: *identity*.

Of interest to me here is the interplay of the psychoanalytic, discursive, and material dimensions of desire in the production of the schooled subject. Further, as an educator, my focus is twofold: the disciplinary, schooling effects of all educational practices; and the disciplinary effects of all schooling practices. McLaren (1994), following on Paulo Freire and Henry Giroux, distinguishes between schooling and education: "the former is primarily a mode of social control; the latter has the potential to transform society, with the learner functioning as an active subject committed to self and social empowerment" (173). Yet both schooling and education are disciplinary. While schooling is more obviously recognizable as an institution of social control and regulation, education, too—albeit differently and to different ends—has a regulatory dimension. Both schooling and education are discursive; both trade in discursive forms and practices. As such, both schooling and education position subjects to desire in particular ways. Both effect the structuring of human desire, albeit with different intents and different effects.

■ A Pedagogy of Desire

Teaching and learning unfold in the register of desire.
—Joanne Pagano (1990, 81)

In the second half of the twentieth century, many pedagogies were developed to intervene in and to counter the cultural and structural hegemonies of contemporary life: critical, feminist, libratory, antiracist, etc. Many of these pedagogies were foundational and drew on concepts inherited through modernist (Enlightenment, Cartesian) thought. In fewer places has the rationalist basis of such pedagogies been more seriously challenged and eroded than in the literature that asserts the important connections among desire, power, knowledge, and subjectivity. Such postmodernist critiques of reason, objectivity, universality, essence, and progress—the pillars of modernist thought—forged through poststructural modes of analysis, highlighted the complexities of human desire, its cultural representations, and its multiple maneuvres of, and ranges of impact on, the human subject. As noted earlier, psychoanalytic, discursive, and material notions of desire provide insights into and raise questions about the workings of desire, which urge the reconsideration of the grounds from which we proceed, in the invention of what I will term radical pedagogies[4]—pedagogies designed to intervene in and counter the oppressive hegemonies of contemporary life. As desire is implicated in the maintenance of such hegemonies (Davies 1990; Christian-Smith 1993; Walkerdine 1990; Coward 1985; Gilbert and Taylor 1990), so, too, is desire mobilized in the project of transgression.

Such insights form the basis of some of the more exciting developments now available to those who work within radical pedagogies. Approaching pedagogy as a form of cultural politics, recognizing its work on numerous sites and through a wide array of texts, and identifying educators as cultural workers (and cultural workers as educators)—ideas elaborated rigorously by Roger Simon (1992), Henry Giroux (1990), and others—provide an enabling theoretical framework within which to articulate a pedagogy that attempts to address the intersections of knowledge, power, and desire.

Enabling such address means moving beyond dominant notions of pedagogy as skills-based practice. Supplanting such a technicist definition captures the social and political visions that pedagogy relationally engages and forwards. As Roger Simon (1992) notes, "talk about pedagogy is simultaneously talk about the details of what students and teachers might do together *and* the cultural politics such practices support" (57). As Henry Giroux (1994) argues, pedagogy is ultimately about "the creation of a public sphere" (x) through "the production of knowledge, identities, social relations and values that takes place in a variety of cultural sites" (155). Central to such conceptions of pedagogy is a theory of the human subject formed within language and representation, subjected to (as well as a subject of) cultural meaning—the very subject shaped in and through the machinations of pedagogy.

Fundamental to the notion of "subjectivity"—as opposed to that of the "individual," the rational, knowing being born of the Enlightenment and believed capable of full consciousness, a notion that dominates modernist thought—is attention to the unconscious, as well as the conscious, in the constitution of identity. The thinking, feeling, speaking subject, then, is never fully revealed or ever fully knowable to itself—a condition of the simultaneity of consciousness and language. As well, the never fully fixed or stable position of the subject within language guarantees that subjectivity is always in process and that a subject is ever capable of occupying multiple, oftentimes contradictory, subject positions within, albeit regulatory but never fully closed, discourses. In this sense, the subject is a condition of signification; and, the conditions or workings of signification are the conditions of the (re)making of the subject.

A poststructural pedagogy premises its work on this notion of subjectivity. Since such a pedagogy is centered on the struggle over the constitutive and constituting character of language, discourse, and meaning, it is, de facto, centered on the subject. Inasmuch as pedagogy targets the subject, whether acknowledged or not, it does and must contend with the unconscious. Given these connections, radical pedagogies necessarily participate in the struggle over language, representation, and meaning as social *and* psychic struggles, as irrational and indeterminable practices. Where language is the condition and the conditioner of desire, any pedagogy that centers language, of necessity, centers desire. In these connections—among pedagogy, language, and desire— are the bases for a pedagogy of desire, a place from which to address pedagogy as design on identity and desire.

This notion of a pedagogy of desire extends "a pedagogy of pleasure and meaning" (Giroux and Simon 1989, 1) or a "pedagogy of desire" (Dyson 1994, 119), each of which attempts to trace and to articulate the formative dynamics of engagement with popular cultural forms (see Chapter 4).[5] In both of these examples, the obvious pleasures of the popular demand an account of the "mobilization of desire" (Giroux 1994, 278) so that the pedagogical workings of the popular can be better understood. In the notion of a pedagogy of desire that I am putting forth, however, these questions are foremost: How are the workings of desire operative within any given pedagogical practice? How, and for what, is the educational gaze desiring? On any and every educational site, in what ways do knowledge, power, desire, and pedagogy intersect and impact at the level of the subject? In what ways are these effects limiting and/or enabling of the crucial issue of "in what direction to desire" (Giroux and Simon 1989, 25)?

It is important to center desire in pedagogy in this way for at least three reasons: The issue of desire galvanizes the major problematics for a radical pedagogy—it struggles with the hegemonies of certain social and psychic patterns; attention to desire also urges a revisiting of the thorny issue of the relationship of psychoanalysis and pedagogy;[6] and, the explicit articulation of the relationship of desire and pedagogy urges the naming and interrogation of other complex and difficult dimensions of our pedagogies, for example, the intersections of pedagogy, identity, and sexual difference (Lewis 1993; Rockhill 1991, 1993). In these ways, then, desire is provocative. As desire refuses a mind/body split, its focus urges attention to embodiment and heightens the sense of psychic and social risk entailed in the work of pedagogy.

▪

The interconnections of the preceding sections reveal the many fronts on which the discussions of the following chapters occur. A fundamental informing premise woven throughout is that schooling practices, i.e., curriculum, pedagogy, etc., produce cultural effects. Situating schooling practices as forms of cultural politics entails recognizing the ways in which such practices operate as established, institutionalized, and ritualized modes of regulation, the resting place of which is embodied subjectivity. This *body of culture*—the broader processes and practices through which it is constituted—is the central concern of the chapters that follow.

Figure 1

	Modernism	Postmodernism	Structuralism	Poststructuralism
Origins	art, architecture, literature, science, social philosophy	art, architecture, film, literature, philosophy	linguistics, literature, anthropology, sociology, psychology	literary theory, feminist philosophy, feminist psychoanalysis
Key writers	Hegel, Marx, Freud, Arnold, Habermas, Dewey, Nietzsche	Lyotard, Jameson, Baudrillard, Rorty, Giroux, Aronowitz, Grossberg, Simon, Haraway, Nicholson	de Saussure, Frye, Levi- Strauss, Jakobson, Piaget, Pierce, Benveniste, Barthes	Derrida, Foucault, Lacan, Kristeva, Cherryholmes, Weedon, Davies
Key characteristics and concepts	Meta/grand/master narratives of Truth, progress, civilization, universality, and order; focus on rationality, reason, and objectivity; unity, order, and control a premise of freedom; essential, unified subject; knowledge as foundational	challenge to modernism; focus on difference/Other, multiplicity, and partiality; anti-foundational perspective on knowledge; focus on culture and representation within late capitalism; implosion, hyper-reality, heteroglossia, simulacrum, and remapping as facets of image-centric culture;	transcendental signifiers and hierarchized meanings; systemic interrelationships of signs; binaries; socially structured sets of differences	rewriting of structuralism; deconstruction, difference and the discourse of the Other; inter-relationship of discourse, power, and subjectivity; instability and materiality of meaning; arbitrary relationship of signs; political production of truth effects; historicity as basis of meaning;

	Modernism	Postmodernism	Structuralism	Poststructuralism
Key characteristics and concepts (continued)		collapse of hierarchies of culture; parody, pastiche, irony as dominant forms of cultural commentary; fragmented, contradictory subject		import of unconscious and impossibility of full self-knowing; contingent identity; critical engagement
Forms/Types	traditional/classical; progressive	ludic; resistance		feminist
Curriculum	authoritative texts; orthodoxies; common goals; child (as resource)-centered	popular meanings; hybrid textualities	systemization; conventions; classifications; application; assessment outcomes; taxonomies	sets of discourses; textual interrogation of discourses and "readings"; modes of critique
Pedagogy	authoritative; transmission; elitist; progressive	border pedagogy; cultural pedagogy; pedagogy of representation; post-critical	technicist; banking/transmission; prescriptive; behavioristic; regulatory; focus on skills, methods, strategies	discourse-centered; post-critical (concern with how subjectivities are produced in/through knowledge/power relations–pedagogy); self-reflexive; problematizing of certainty; making visible coercive quality of texts
Literacy	functional; cultural; progressive	multi-mediated literacies; readings as textual play; postmodern literacies	functional; cultural; progressive; critical	poststructural–critical (reading positions; readings as ventriloquic; constitutive effects of discourse and power on subjectivities)

	Modernism	Postmodernism	Structuralism	Poststructuralism
Feminism	essential femininity– gynocentric; focus on gender	gender as drag, masquerade	sex/gender distinction; sex as basis of structuring of social relations	deconstruction and reconstruction of constitutive forms of femininity; sexual difference as linguistic and material
Criticisms	elitist; oppressive; colonizing; hostile to difference	nihilistic; relativistic; some forms seen as ethically and politically uncommitted	abstract; non-agenic; falsified consensus	tyranny of fragmentation of self; non-agenic; politically suspect

Two

WORD AND FLESH

Language,[1] *Text, and the Incarnation of Desire*[2]

To use language is always to seize the world in a particular way, and at the same time to be seized. To teach language is never to dwell in a sanctuary free from questions of power, but to labour in its smithy. Questions of language are never merely neutral epistemological questions, but are always linked to a whole discursive cluster (notions of representation, meaning, value, subjectivity) whose boundaries trace the limits of our social space and its relational possibilities.

—Robert Morgan (1987, p.457)

The body is the central relay point—the *point d'appui*—in the dialectical reinitiation of meaning and desire.

—Peter McLaren (1995, p.63)

■ This chapter furthers the discussion of language begun in the first chapter. In Chapter 1, a theoretical interrelationship of language, culture, power, desire, and identity was sketched to provide the conceptual groundwork for a discussion of the cultural politics of literacy practices. In this chapter, issues of the embodied character of knowledge and meaning are presented to highlight the centrality of the body as the work site of language and, therefore, of literacy practices. If literacy practices frame how the social world is negotiated and understood—meaning as social relations—then literacy practices demarcate the body and its *sign*-ificance within the social. If discourses of desire (w)rest on the body, through subjectivity, then, the body can be understood as a signifier of desire.

■ **Embodied Literacies**

The intimate relationship between discourse and subjectivity meet at the workplace of language—the site of construction of subjectivity in all its dimensions—the body. The opening quote from Robert Morgan reiterates this point through its use of verbs—seize, labor, dwell—that center the bodily work of, the body at work in, the body worked through language. Yet, cast against traditions that align language and thought—and, therefore, language and the mind—and that separate mind and body, efforts to articulate the embodiment of language bear the dual burden of resisting these (and other) dangerous dualisms while claiming the body as a political space inhabited (colonized) and regulated by language. Complicating these efforts are widely circulating common-sense notions of language as a technicist *tool*; these notions promote a sense of language as acquisitional, a commodity, which can be used for purposes of one's choosing. Language is, indeed, related to what its users can do, but in ways more complex and, even, more insidious than commonsense accounts reveal. As that by which the meaning of existence is represented, nothing escapes the mediating stroke of language. In this sense, the parameters of who we are—socially, culturally, bodily—come into existence through, and are shaped by, particular language practices.[3]

In an attempt to reassert the importance of embodiment and to point to the schooling—the disciplining effects of knowledge practices—Madeleine Grumet (1992) notes pointedly that "[e]ducation always refers to the development of some-body" (36). Similarly, Magda Lewis (1993) calls for "the concrete articulation of a body knowledge" (54), an awareness, in Lewis's case, of how dominant discursive practices position women subordinately. Peter McLaren (1995) reiterates this point of these and other feminists while also seizing on the irresponsibility of schools vis-à-vis this point:

> The problem with schools is not that they ignore bodies, their pleasures, and the suffering of the flesh (although admittedly this is part of the problem) but that they undervalue language and representation as constitutive factors in the shaping of body/subject as the bearer of meaning, history, race, and gender. (69)

Language, as that through which knowledge is constructed and educational experiences and schooling practices mediated, is the primary focus of a project of *body language*—the body as signifying; the project addresses how language is constitutive of an embodied subjectivity and how discourses, in the Foucaultian sense of language structures of power and governance, are always discourses of the body, the site on which meanings of identity, difference, desire, knowledge, social worth, and possibility are assimilated and contested. Reformulating the project of education and schooling through these notions of language and consequence contests the very foundations of educational order.

The regulation of bodies has historically been a primary focus of the project of education. A range of social practices has been and continues to be the means to this accomplishment, and none more so than language practices. How language is understood, then, has immense implications for how experiences and meanings are conceived and the extent to which personal and collective agency can affect—challenge, contest, and (re)configure—them. However, a conscious sense of the extent to which language and discourse regulate desiring bodies remains largely outside the everyday foci of schooling and educational practices. What this chapter seeks to explore is the basis of a poststructural theory of language that does not distance itself from the embodied subject of language,[4] and the challenges and opportunities such a notion of language offers educational practice, in particular, practices concerned with challenging current hegemonies.

■ Desire and/in Language

Discursive, material, and psychoanalytic dimensions of desire are each implicated in and concerned with language and its structuring effects on the human subject. For feminists, the most contentious of these is psychoanalytic notions of desire and language. Some poststructural feminists reject psychoanalytic notions of desire because of their essentialization of femininity within, and the phallogocentricism of, the dominant discourses of psychoanalysis, within which, typically, "woman" is positioned in terms of lack, absence, and difference. Such theorists claim, both implicitly and explicitly, that language and desire are inextricably bound and it is by attending to the discursive and manifest workings of desire, in and through, for example, an array of social texts, that is most productive (Davies 1990). This argument, while politically focused, manifests rationalist leanings that ignore the erratic character of desire and the irrevocable character of unknowing that accompanies human action.[5] Attending critically to the insights of psychoanalysis not only heightens our sense of these discursive complexities but also provides guideposts for proceeding pedagogically.

The extensive work of Valerie Walkerdine (1990) in representing the mutual rootedness of the social and the psychic is convincing in its argument that it is at our peril that we encourage analyses that attempt to separate social and psychic realities, so imbued is one with the other. From a poststructural perspective, to attend only to the structuring effects on subjectivity of desire and/in language can be to ignore the psychic fantasies out of which such positions are produced and the psychic struggles through which such discursive positions are accepted, rejected, modified, accommodated. Discursive practices, in this sense, can be said "to channel psychic conflicts and contradictions in particular ways" (Walkerdine 1990, 103) so that it is possible to view dreams, desires, and wishes as products of the engagement of the psychic and the social. More useful understandings, for socially transformative purposes, of the forms of engagement of such practices involve attempting to come to terms with the nature of both the psyche and the social, in their mutually constitutive ways. In the work of the social, in the structuring of desire in language, discourse, and representation, there is also the structuring of the psyche, that which lies beneath language but not out of its reach. From a psychoanalytic perspective, this structuring is two-way in that the psyche, through the mechanism of desire, locates itself, always incompletely and ineffectually, in discourse.

The convergence of language and psychoanalysis has its most provocative roots in the psychoanalytic theory of Jacques Lacan, of whom rereadings, many of which are feminist, have shaped much current cultural and social theory.[6] Lacan argues that the unconscious is formed upon our entry into language as speaking subjects, the moment at which the distinction between the speaking subjects "I" and "You" is realized. In this realization is the beginning emergence, through language, of subjectivity, gendering, and the creation of repressed desire and the unconscious. Because the creation of the unconscious is simultaneous with the entry into language and the repression of desire, Lacan argues that the unconscious is structured like a language and, therefore, to speak language is to speak repressed desire for a lost unity. Toril Moi (1985) highlights Lacan's debt to the French linguist Ferdinand de Saussure[7] in her comments on this insight of Lacan into the shared qualities of the unconscious and language:

> [D]esire "behaves" in precisely the same way as language: it moves ceaselessly on from object to object or from signifier to signifier, and will never find full and present satisfaction just as meaning can never be seized as full presence. . . . There can be no

final satisfaction of our desire since there is no final signifier or object that can be that which has been lost forever (the imaginary harmony with the mother and the world). (101)

From this insight can be understood the renegotiation of desire as a resignifying project, the grounds for which are established in other compelling aspects of this argument: its attention to language as the crucible of desire; its suggestion of dissatisfaction as a perpetual condition of consciousness (and of language use and meaning); and, through these, the presentation of ripe ground for discursive challenges and change. Without the condition of dissatisfaction, change has no grounds in which to sow, for its seeds thrive in the grounds of discontent. The condition of discontent, in Lacanian terms, is contemporaneous with entry into language. Desire, the manifestation of discontent, is, then, what links the unconscious into language, as a culturally bound, always unstable, and contested signifier. It is to this condition that Elizabeth Wright (1984) refers in her claim, regarding Lacan's theory, that "[t]here is an incessant struggle within language, because it is at once cause and effect of the body's desire" (176). In this sense, as Kaja Silverman (1983) notes, "the subject not only learns to desire within the symbolic order; it learns *what* to desire" (177–8).

The instability of the psyche, which such an account captures, is best marked in the displacement of desire onto unattainable fantasies of wholeness and satisfaction accessed through the social. In this sense, the social acts pedagogically in that it proffers the illusion of satisfaction while banking on inevitable absence and dissatisfaction, and, in its processes, offers subject positions with which to identify and from which subjects may feel in control of desire—the materialization of the illusion. The impossibility of this fulfillment, this control, and any conscious awareness of such impossibility, have no hold, for it is in the desire to be whole, to be in control, borne of language as we are born into language, that propels us to continue the chase. In the movement through the social, its signifiers and their attendant fantasies, sites of pleasure, ways of being pleasurable, pleasing, and pleased—and their antecedents—are earmarked again and again. It is in the active production of subjectivity within the signifying practices of the social through which configurations of difference—gender, social class, race, and sexuality—are embedded. (Not fixed, but embedded.) However, thinking ourselves in control of our desires, our meanings, our language, subjects live the illusion of a choice unabated by the confines of a symbolic order constructed on the grounds of gross inequities and with which our established patterns or habits of desire can and do collude: the problem of desire (Davies 1990).

This problem of desire is deeply compounded on pedagogical sites; in particular, those pedagogical sites—schools, colleges, and universities, specifically—forged out of and surrounded by the throws of rationality and self-evidentiality. What is on offer as knowledge on these sites is often bereft of any attention to the psychic and political character of the embodiment of knowledge and the vested interests, at the level of desire, of both teachers and students. This repression is accentuated by the ways in which both teachers and students are positioned into rationality, despite what we may claim to know and feel otherwise. While here I address these issues largely within the context of my work, as a student and, now, as a teacher of graduate education, I see the structuring of desire to be central to any and all educational efforts.

■ Body Language: Or, Words-Matter

I don't want to be made of words and feelings. I don't want to be a body that craves.

—Roo Borson (in Fagan 1995)

Written on the body is a secret code only visible in certain lights; the accumulations of a lifetime gather there. In places the palimpsest is so heavily worked that the letters feel like braille.

—Jeanette Winterson (1992, 89)

Over a decade ago, amidst my graduate studies, I experienced profoundly and deeply what I described then as a crisis of language. As I articulated it then, I could no longer adequately (sanely?) maneuvre in the gap between what my body spoke to me—what I felt and understood in my body—and what I could represent in words: a profound sense that *there are no words for it*.[8] This feeling was not new, but the intensity of it, and the measure of bodily dis-ease that accompanied it, was. This experience forms the basis from which to think through what for me are two interrelated issues: the embodied character of the relationship of language and subjectivity; and the ongoing debates around poststructural accounts of subjectivity and what are often referred to as identity politics—where or to what extent it is politically viable or theoretically defensible to position oneself within a claim to, disdain for,

and/or erasure of, a habitually named, if not fixed and therefore essentialized, identity polity.

The crisis of language to which I refer occurred as I was beginning
to immerse myself in poststructural writings. But I was to experience
the embodied effects of poststructural theories (and at the hands of
poststructural theories) long before I had acquired a fuller grasp of the
major tenets of the theory. I now see the experience to which I refer as
a crisis of subjectivity—but no less a crisis of language—was forged
within the regimes of graduate schooling. Its effects were, and are still,
felt as not only discursive, but also as psychically, bodily, and socially
disruptive. I initially described the crisis as one of language—as *opposed*
to subjectivity—because, at the time, I could not fully articulate what I
embodied, that my identity, my sense of self/selves, constituted in and
through language, and what it was possible for me to say in defense of
that assemblage, was in question. Previous to this experience, I had seen
language as related to (my) identity only in the ways in which a social
model of language (see chapter 1) allowed. In other words, I saw the
relationship of language and identity as representative and representing
but not constitutive and constituting.

What I read as a crisis, then, I now read as the tumultuous, disturbing, disrupting, threatening, and sometimes even joyous but definitely
very embodied reality of the theoretical *subject positioned within discourse*,
a position in which dimensions of my subjectivity were unravelling so
that desire might be rethreaded. However, this acceptance of the necessary fragmentation of the poststructural subject-as-lived came after
the experience of "the dictatorship of the fragment" (Best, in Mclaren
1994, 207) as violation. If one cannot or does not name oneself as split,
fragmented, and contradictory—a mystifying effect of modernist ideologies of identity—to reconsider oneself through such a poststructural
lens can be traumatic and disruptive, as well as potentially liberating.
Issuing its own regulatory effects, such protestations felt impossible to
say beyond the contained, restrained position of silence as a mask for
ill-fit.

This cloak of silence to which I refer lingers throughout my history;
it is a *leitmotif* of my schooling experiences in particular. Consistently,
through many—often feminist—accounts of silence, specifically those
that correlate silence and voicelessness, I have struggled against a position wherein my own silence was abstracted and politicized outside the
terms of my own practice of that very silence. My silence was more in
keeping with what Magda Lewis (1993) calls "silence born of dissent"

(3). It was a silence of refusal, a means by which to remember, to hold fast to what one discursive position strives to erase in another. Through poststructural theories, I encountered, paradoxically, a silencing that would break the silence, the war of wordlessness turned out-word.

Graduate study is as threatening as it is exciting. Within an institutional ethos in which (often competing) discourses—feminisms, Marxism, deconstruction, liberal humanism, etc.—not only position students differently but also compete for their loyalties, both inside and outside the classroom, discursive coercion is an implicit character of daily life,[9] an aspect of compartmental, departmental, and/or overall institutional identity-building. I came to such an institutional context with an extremely strong sense of cultural identity, specially constituted around regional place, and what I would describe as a theoretically unevolved but deeply felt sense of social justice. Given that these two characteristics were not necessarily incompatible, indeed, in many ways were very compatible, why was it that I experienced so much difficulty reconciling the two? How was it that my theoretical evolution around the bases of social (in)justice that was part of graduate schooling was so alienating, culturally? Why did so many of the ideologies of justice feel such an ill-fit? Why did what should have felt liberating often feel suffocating? Why did what my head know seem so forcefully rejected by, or removed from, my body, to the extent that self-decapitative, strangling[10] urges—wanting my mind to leave my body alone—abounded? And what might I now learn from the social contradictions created through my various positionings within these discourses that could helpfully inform my own pedagogy?

Some of the answers to these questions lie in the competing claims of identity and the personal and collective desires invested therein. This insight is not new or profound. However, it is one thing to be insightful; it is quite another to monitor the *reali*zation of that insight as it pertains to embodied subjectivities. No discourse, however well deployed in the name of social justice and particularity, is without its normalizing, homogenizing, and aggressive tendencies. In the face of the question—which is the question of the subject in discourse—of *what the discourse into which I am being positioned expects/demands/desires of me as a subject*, the answers may not be straightforward at all. Yet the pedagogical room for maneuvring the answers is often not provided and simply made impossible by the constraints of course duration, lack of collective space for such discussions outside of classes, etc. But, if identity is a set of relational claims continually negotiated within a community as a means to attain solidarity, sustenance, and comfort, old and new identities are not easily or readily renegotiated. A discourse of social justice must necessarily enable that space of renegotiation; the commitments to identity are psychically deep and fulfill real needs, if not necessarily in the most libratory of ways.

Naomi Scheman (1995) discusses the need to reflect on how discourses, the epistemological claims of which may well be exact, can be "problematically coercive" (114) and exacting on those who are positioned within their influence. Oppositional discourses that suffer poor exchange rates against dominant currency depend on a certain "bunker mentality" to maintain solidarity and effective struggle. As a result, any critique of internal coercion is often ignored, dismissed, ridiculed, and/or bullied offstage rather than examined for what it reveals about the limits of the discourse that hails itself as libratory. And rather than recognize how the posing of limits can enhance the grounds of further possibility, critique is also often received as, itself, limited and, therefore, dismissable.[11] But what is a feminism that is not rooted in the everyday maneuvres and negotiations by women of culture and the many competing dimensions, of place, class, ethnicity, race, spiritual conviction, sexuality, etc., that constitute the "locatedness" of those maneuvres? What is a pedagogy that sidesteps its own impacts as it designs itself around notions of language, power, and subjectivity? How can a project of enablement succeed through practices, the effects of which can register as so alienating, so disabling? The worth of the projects of such discourses creates an urgency around responses to such questions, and it is in keeping with the praxis-oriented stance of such discourses of feminisms and radical pedagogies that maintain the importance of such self-reflexive questions.

In his discussion of "the fear of theory" within the context of graduate schooling, Roger Simon (1992) addresses, in relation to language practices and the organization of social identities, the disruptive potential of theory. Simon locates one source of this disruption as potentially realized in aspects of "self-abandonment," "the potential negation of aspects of one's personal and professional identity and the corresponding investments one has in retaining those identity positions (86). As Simon formulates them, these disruptions can threaten not only professional practices—how one understands and positions oneself as educator—but also how one understands oneself as part of a cultural community when that community is subordinated through relations of power based on, for example, class, ethnicity, gender, and race. Threats to belonging resonate in the most vulnerable corners of our psyches, whether it is the threat one feels as a woman in academia, a lesbian in a small community, or a student whose desires and longings do not match the rhythm of the pedagogical project at hand. But there is also another issue here. Identity may well not be fixed, but the vehemence of the claim to it and its bodily resonances suggest, at the least, a deeply held conviction, a political claim, that cannot be deconstructed without embodied *psychic* and social implications. There is a toll exacted on identity by theory that offers few alternates to disruption, fragmentation, and, therefore, political immobilization. Such theory threatens to mock conviction with abstractions and tourist models of structures of feeling.

Part of what I perceive in the struggles *within* the (often competing) discourses of feminisms, radical pedagogies, postcolonialisms, etc., is a plea for a space of representation that those for whom a discourse claims to speak may call *home*.[12] A notion of home must surely be unpopular, and certainly problematic, in these days of postmodern nomads and travelling pedagogues. By home I mean that place within discourse(s) of/and representation where the identities that nurture, console, support, and give life to us might still have a respect and a validity. This home is not easily created; its frame is the strength of difference. The desire for such a home may well come from a residue subject not quite postmodern, formed in one of the spaces of what Carmen Luke (1993) calls "the vast social and geographic terrain who cannot be rightly labelled as either culturally modernist or postmodernist" (192) and who still clings to that aspect of self. The "enforced fragmentation" of social and cultural life, what McRobbie (1994, 23) argues accounts for the appeal of postmodernism for the young and/or disenfranchised, is lived specifically, by degrees and difference, across a range of cultural fronts. The urges of a wide array of subjects must be addressed within a project of social justice, for its desires reach into and stake claims on many who want to change their homes, not abandon them fully.

Neither is the desire for such a home a claim of essence. As strong as my sense of place is, when I name myself under its cultural signifier I do so variably. It is a sign of imperialist arrogance that the complexity and variance of this practice of naming should be so reduced. Part of the threat my graduate studies held for me was a dismissal and/or dissolution of that identity as those same studies also offered me the space and the means to reconfigure and to claim other, also marginalized aspects of my identity. Herein is my point: If we accept the conditions of language as constitutive and constituting, we must necessarily locate the debate around identity politics in terms of embodied subjectivity and the dynamics of threat and desire therein. What is it that a particular subordinate social group is unwilling to relinquish to the poststructural version of the subject? What is it that the poststructural version of the subject resists, bypasses, overlooks? In whose interests has this subject emerged? Is it possible that the theoretical hegemony of the nomadic subject has formed its own exclusions?

Finally, is there a way to avoid discursive violence while also pursuing the project of "transforming the subject"? Judith Williamson (1981/2) identifies this problem with startling clarity, yet there is little evidence in the literature to date to suggest that educational language practices have adjusted to this often-reiterated insight. Instead, the serious grounds for questioning the "hacking at the very roots" (85) of identity has been replaced by a cavalier attitude toward the very constitution of the subject itself. If it is all pastiche, fragment, surface—hack away! Within the postmodern, display threatens to replace embodiment and desire flirts with the (un)real. As Peter McLaren (1995) notes, "[b]y locating the subject within the surface meaning of the image and by making our subjectivities so malleable, postmodern culture contributes unwittingly to the demise and depoliticization of the historical subject" (60). Finally, admitting that I was "made of words" was tantamount to the collapse of the house of cards, or to the revelation that the emperor had no clothes. Weaned on the dominant view of language as possibility, the domain of beauty, and self-designated, through a career choice to teach English, to promulgate "the Word," the more shocking "truths" about language (to say nothing of those about English teaching) were shocking, indeed.

However, the certainties that hold us intact—to which we lay claim in identity—are not necessarily, or in all ways, ill-founded. Finding a place from which to investigate this position—my doctoral research—returned to me, with an enlarged vision and a renewed vigor, that place called home. Mapping the broad terrain of (my own) subjectivity—its production and productions—not only allowed me to rest in the irresolve of my crisis of language; it also pointed me toward a reconceptualized notion of teaching, at the heart of which are issues of language, power, desire, and subjectivity. In part, this redirection was facilitated through a confrontation of my own desires, that is, a direct address of the crisis of language *cum* subjectivity, through the discourses of feminism, psychology, history, political economy, and literary theory, in an effort to enhance the project of becoming, to the extent that it is possible, the subject of my own desires.

If it is the (often unstated) purpose of schooling to mould and meld citizen desire, I would argue that it is the project of a radical pedagogy not only to identify this process, but to provide the opportunity to address the collective and often contradictory investments that are identity and the particular embodiment of identity-as-desire as constitutive engagements with/in the social. Yet, if "the network which is the subject is made up of the properties of language" (Coward and Ellis 1977, 107), then any deconstruction of meaning—the site on which the subject speaks—is practiced on the body. Peter McLaren (1995) captures the relationship in his notion of enfleshment:

> [Ideas] are enfleshed in ideologies and historical and cultural forms of subjectivity. Enfleshment can be conceived here as the mutually constitutive aspect (enfolding) of social structure and desire. Discourses neither sit on the surface of the flesh nor float about in the formless ether of the mind but are enfolded into the very structures of our desire inasmuch as desire itself is formed by the anonymous historical rules of discourse. It is in this sense, then, that the body/subject becomes *both the medium and the outcome of subjective formation.* (67–8)

The relationship of language and desire is pivotal to an understanding of the formation of the subject and any pedagogical project designed to change the subject.

■ Language Practices for the (In)Subordinate[13]

If it is the case that our very entry into language, the symbolic order, is a interminable moment of alienation, as was pointed out earlier in the chapter in the discussion of Lacanian theory, and if this alienation is more so for some than others, depending on how one is positioned—privileged and/or denied—within the structure of the symbolic order, then educational practices defined through language must necessarily strive to ease, and not to exacerbate, that alienation. A different relationship to language is a different relationship to desire. Joanne Pagano (1990) notes the moral imperative of education in relation to these differences language makes for women:

> We cannot assume that men and women are in a position to know the same things since their relationship to language, to the spectral body and to the body politic are different. Since education has everything to do with our finding our positions in language, education must treat men and women differently within the range of the common interest which defines the educational project. (68)

Pagano's point suggests not only the profound sociality of language but, also, the embodied character of that sociality—the sociality of the embodied self-in-language. This point is reiterated by Gates (1985) in his description of the "relation of indenture" (13) in which Blacks find themselves with language.

> Who has seen a black or red person, a white, yellow or brown? These terms are arbitrary constructs, not reports of reality. But language is not only the medium of this often insidious tendency; it is its *sign*. Current language use signifies the difference between cultures and their possession of power, spelling out the distance between subordinate and superordinate . . . in terms of their race. (6)

The points made by both Pagano and Gates highlight the profound neglect of girls and women, and subordinate groups generally, within dominant educational language practices. It is to issues of language practice surrounding this neglect that I wish to address my points in this section.

The interrelationship of language, desire, discourse, and power, as they have been articulated here and in Chapter 1, urges an address of the educational implications of the inequities inherent in its formulation and practices. Given their constituency in and through language, the discourses out of which are formed educational philosophies and pedagogical practices in no small or exemptive ways, *court students' desires*. Within the current context of language studies, issues of language, power, desire and subjectivity are generally ignored, and structural and social models of language abound to the near exclusion of other more disruptive models. What such educational circumstance means is that what is on offer to students—implicitly and explicitly— amounts to partial (in both senses of the word) and misleading social visions that testify to the failure of desire in its dominant configurations. Failing to account for and confront the constitutive character of language—to refuse to problematize how language practices court desire and constitute identity—can become, for many, a case of desire often courting disaster. Gates (1985) provides a disturbing and revealing case in point in his story of the Haitian writer Edmond Laforest, who tied a dictionary to his neck and then leapt to his death, an act Gates interprets as a symbolic gesture of the "overwhelming indenture" (1985, 13) of the marginalized to language. The everyday quieter and less often noticed disasters that occur in classrooms may not hold the drama of this story but they nevertheless speak profound and embodied violation only deepened when ignored or taken for granted. Recasting educational practices in favor of those disadvantaged by its dominant workings requires a politics of language and practice that not only challenges and but is also more dissonant than that of widespread contemporary practices.

Despite the currency of so-called back-to-basics arguments, language practices within education—in particular in Canada, the United States, the United Kingdom, and Australia—often embrace process-oriented practices, the most common of which is termed whole language.[14] While the focus of most whole language scholarship addresses its efficacy and use in primary and elementary school contexts, its impact can be seen in educational practices from primary to tertiary schooling, in formal and informal settings and in public, private, and adult educational contexts. Characterized by literature-based instruction, personal response, learner-constructed materials, and process-writing approaches, whole language practices are designed to address the whole learner in the whole context of learning. Juxtaposed with a skills-based approach to language development and use, whole language leans on naturalistic, noncoercive approaches to competency in language. Whole language practices usually coexist with student-centered pedagogy and a curriculum based in liberal humanist ideology.[15] (See Figure 1, Chapter 1.) In this sense, then, whole language can be said to form a set of practices that envision a particular form of what Robert Morgan (1990) calls *school literacy*. "School literacy constitutes a second, State-sponsored linguistic birth, an attempt to make 'second-nature' particular orientations to society and self through the agency of schooled language" (204).

Adherents of whole language often point, as a strength, to its emphasis on the important connection of language, meaning, and identity. However, many, if not most, whole language practices tend to reflect an insipid, seemingly apolitical approach to the implications of this very connection. A language philosophy characterized by such emphasis as that of whole language would seem, of necessity—to say nothing of the necessity of rigor—to espouse an understanding of language as productive, constitutive, and, therefore, socially *regulative*, that is, a theory that acknowledged the political basis of language. Instead, whole language practices tend to reflect a notion of language as expressive, personal, and transparent (Morgan 1987, 450) and, in so doing, leave intact a misleading self-evidence about language that denies the work of ideology therein. Nowhere within whole language practices is this more evident than in the widespread talk of individual authenticity of voice and experience, as if these characteristics could exist outside the social context of language usage and already circulating meanings. In this sense, whole language practices fall short of what John Willinsky (1990) calls their "best intentions." Frances Christie (1993), in her critique of the related (individual) growth model of English teaching, succinctly captures the problem:

> [T]he "growth model" . . . promised more than it could ever really deliver. . . . There were, broadly, two reasons for this: First, the "growth model" had an essentially romantic notion of the individual, conceived in some idealized sense as "growing" while developing personally important meanings, and it failed to acknowledge the social nature of human existence. Second, and for related reasons, in that the model focused primarily on persons constructing their own meanings in an idealized way, its effect was to deflect attention from the nature of language itself. (77)

Touting apparently depoliticized notions of student ownership of language and authenticity of expression and meaning, and reducing power itself to notions of personal esteem, whole language educators, across a wide spectrum of educational sites and practices, can and often do participate in the silent but assured regeneration of the social status quo. In such contexts, where social power is only apparently nullified and where its social intricacies and insidiousness—what is not necessarily self-evident about language—are ignored, socially disenfranchised students can be left to write themselves and their texts with little or no attention to the ways in which they, themselves, and others, are *written by* these texts, and by language generally. Such practices cannot embrace a pedagogy of reflective desire, one in which the constitutive character of subjectivity in language is a focus. One consequence of such subversion of power is that many students can and often do literally and pleasurably speak, write, and read themselves into the available—often, the dominant—discursive positions of subordination and (in)difference.

However, it is not only such writings, in and of themselves, that are problematic. What is more problematic is the lack of interrogation of such writings as effects of the preponderance of certain social discourses, the dearth of pleasurable alternatives, and how both conditions reflect issues of power. Another consequence, as Gemma Moss (1989) suggests, is that without such interrogation and critique, it is impossible to reap a fuller potential for students of their own writings, which, themselves, are often deeply contradictory texts of struggle and mean-ing-negotiation. In her study of the writing of young girls, Moss cites examples of young females in whose writings wrest their struggles with accommodating heterosexual romance while simultaneously resisting domination by boyfriends. Access to the implications of such accom-modations of and resistances to the gendered social order are not avail-able without an overt, proactive approach to the relationship of social politics and language study.

Whole language practices, made more compelling by their celebra-tion of modernist notions of the individual within educational contexts that often value student-centered pedagogy, work effectively as a form of social regulation. What I am arguing is that centering the individual as meaning-maker *extraordinaire* displaces the impact of social (dis)orders of patriarchy, capitalism, and white supremacy on the pro-duction and reproduction of meaning. To continue to perpetuate such inflated autonomy in meaning-making and to ignore or to efface the relationship of language, social power, and identity—to ignore how dis-courses can promote or challenge current hegemonies—is to partici-pate in the socialization of students into an unwitting collusion with these (dis)orders. If language is the "always already" bearer of sociality, then the ways in which students are borne of and participate in this sociality requires full attention in institutions that claim to be educa-tional. If, as Robert Morgan (1990) claims, the curriculum subject Eng-lish (and, I would argue, schooling, generally) is "a training in how to say 'I'" (203), a critical literacy has to begin here.

The dominance within education of whole language and student-centered practices poses a daunting obstacle to the improved quality of the educational experiences of subordinate groups generally. Both whole language practices and student-centered pedagogy tend to employ an acritical approach to notions of selfhood. With their empha-sis on active, responsive, and assertive learning as process, with an ever-evolving rational, responsible, and unique individual as their desired product, whole language and student-centered pedagogy offer as their most likely discursive position an "implied student," the social being who, within the present social order, has the greater chances of embodying such characteristics—a White, bourgeois male. Further, within student-centered pedagogy and whole language practices, stu-dents are seen as knowers, active producers, and makers of meaning, with far less attention given to the ways in which we are all actively reproduced, *are made*, in and through language usage. My point is that students are both makers of meaning and are made by meaning; *both* of these conditions of meaning-making require emphasis in the language classroom. It is not an either/or circumstance; acknowledgement of the complex nature of language in our lives demands close scrutiny of both its ventriloquic effects *as well as* its agenic possibilities.

In the present educational context, in which individualism and personal expression are romanticized, and in which discursive production is downplayed or denied, ignored is the potential embodiment of severe contradictions by students for whom the demands of dominant discourses are often oppositional to these educational desirables of whole language and student-centered pedagogy. The result for such students is that language learning becomes a site of unconscionable struggle. For example, through such practices, often explicitly as well as implicitly, young girls are told to be one thing—active, assertive, and responsive students—while they are also applauded for being quite another—nice, quiet girls; this is but one example of "an act of splitting" (Walkerdine 1990, 46), in which differences are denied, contradictions are effaced, and struggles are subverted. Black students can, likewise, find themselves positioned within a hypocritical notion of activeness, assertiveness, and responsiveness that culturally excludes them. Without issues of language, power, and identity on the agenda of language classrooms, what students can come to know and, more devastatingly, come to accept as the meaning of pleasure, fulfillment, desire, and denial, is a society disordered on the basis of gender, race, social class, and sexual identity and into which they fit in particular ways; they are denied the opportunity to examine how to demand, and live within, a different place in that order. In such circumstances, the relationship of language, power, and identity results in identity as missed opportunity. From this perspective, whole language and student-centered practices, as pedagogy—as strategies and processes that support particular social visions (Simon 1992, 4)—support a social vision of the status quo.

What, then, might be alternative perspectives on pedagogy and curriculum that take seriously the constitutive character of language, the political nature of student experiences and expressions, and, therefore, the sociality of meaning-making? Certainly, the development of curriculum more inclusive of "missing discourses" (Fine 1992), that is, those regimes of meaning actively and systematically excluded from circulation in school, accompanied by a sustained critique of the discursive production of identity, are important aspects of change. However, these changes by themselves are insufficient. As Sandra Taylor (1993) points out, work to dismantle structural inequities must accompany such curricular and pedagogical interventions if they are to be at all effective. Yet even with these necessary changes, the project remains long and deep, for at its heart is a more compelling and more complex task—the renegotiation of desire. If socially disenfranchised students now name as pleasurable their positions within misogynist, racist, and other inequitable discourses, at the very least, it seems necessary to work to name the difficulties that can be incurred in attempting to fit into discursive positions that benefit and please some as they disadvantage and mute others while, at once, attempting what, in reality, can be near futile, often self-destructive and self-effacing efforts to find a dignified pleasure within these oppressive language formations.

The more challenging pedagogical project, then, is one aimed at breaking the nexus between pleasure and powerlessness—the hegemonic construction of desire for women, persons of color, and others. This project can only begin in language classrooms where a pedagogy of desire is named and contested and where both the psychic and social conflicts and contradictions inherent in the embodied workings of desire are confronted as part of the daily making and remaking of meaning. Yet, such language practices must also strive to buffer the kinds of crises to which I referred in the previous section. Discursive coercion may well result in renegotiated desire—but by means embodied not that differently than those of dominant practices.

The beginning place of such a project is in the documentation of experience through auto/biography, narrative, and memory. In particular, auto/biographical writing has become both a prevalent and privileged form of educational practice. Yet, as the next chapter will suggest, the auto/biographical project is not straightforward. The limits and possibilities of auto/biography are largely contingent on the theory of language as well as the complementary theories of self and society that inform its multiple practices.

Three

TELLTALE SIGNS

Auto/biography,[1] Schooling, and the Subject of Desire

■ This chapter addresses the issues surrounding the increasingly widespread use of auto/biographical writing within educational practice. In so doing, it draws on and extends discussions of language, literacy, curriculum and pedagogy as forms of cultural politics and practice. In particular, this chapter locates embodiment and auto/biography as mutually informing versions of social location and literacy practices. That is, herein I strive to make problematic the *body of stories* that both constitute and are constitutive of ways of being literate in the world: auto/biography and/as pedagogy, as desiring practice.

■ Auto/biographical Practice in Context

An apparent paradox has emerged out of the increasing influence of poststructural practice: the intensified attention to auto/biography in education. It is paradoxical in that a genre that has traditionally signaled attention to, and even romanticized, the *individual* of liberal humanist and modernist thinking—the essentialized authentic and rational self (see Chapter 1)—seems an unlikely site of popular practice within a theoretical context in which the constitution of self and the origins and authenticity of its narratives are highly contested. Indeed, the proliferation of auto/biography within curriculum and practice preceded (and continues to supersede) poststructural critical attention to it. Emerging alongside the preponderance of the popular uses of auto/biography in education, however, is a more radical practice, which questions the discursive production of memory, history, representation, desire, and knowledge while addressing head-on the implications of such insights not only for how notions of subjectivity and collectivity are understood but, also, for how pedagogies are mobilized (Lewis 1993; Schenke 1991). Such practice addresses the problematics of versions of self/subject constituted through already written and actively constituting language discourses (see Chapters 1 and 2).

Despite this latter work, auto/biographical writing, as curriculum and practice, from middle school to graduate school, with child and adult learners and in formal and informal educational contexts, continues to be utilized mainly in the dominant forms developed and promoted by the advocates of personal growth and progressive literacy models (see Chapters 1 and 2) who, in turn, drew their modified and non-canonic notions of story, narrative, and auto/biography from the dominant traditions established through the social history of literary genre and mode.[2] Within these models, the production and use of auto/biography is infused with the fundamental premises that inform all other aspects of progressive literacy practices: the *authentic* self exists; through reading, the authentic self is *discovered*; through writing, the authentic self is *expressed*; writing is a *transparent* window to the nature of the authentic self; and, the authentic self is a *maker* of meaning, a forger of *personal* destiny, empowered through access to the *Word*. This notion of the logo-authentic self forms the rationale for (this approach to) literacy. Through such practices, as Gemma Moss (1993) notes,

> [a]utobiography emerges as the privileged text, the ideal space for telling the truth about oneself and evading the kinds of misrepresentation commonplace in popular fiction. . . . Writing is treated as an unmediated revelation of the self. The authors' sense of themselves, their self-worth, can be read off from the text. To judge the writing is to judge the author. (106)

Poststructural theorists challenge the very basis of such practices, from the theory of language that supports them to the conception of self promoted by them.

However, poststructural theories also pose peculiar problems for many theorists and practitioners weaned on earlier notions of the truth of experience, the political necessity of public access to stories, and the collectivity built through shared experiences. For example, these notions were once and are still staples of many forms of feminism but are now contested on the basis of voice, speaking/silencing, and ethnocentrism, which call for renewed visions of what the necessity of building a collectivity across difference might entail. The importance of poststructural theories within these debates is not simply to theorize the cracks in the seams of earlier feminisms but, more importantly, to provide the means for proceeding with identity-(re)shaping practices that challenge monovocalism, unreflective certainties, and ahistorical perspectives. Within a project so defined, where and how the (feminine) subject is positioned is no longer taken for granted; rather, the specifics of location within discourses of history, culture, biology, economics, and schooling are that much more important as a more nuanced and more hopeful project unfolds. Seizing the importance of re-presenting and re-writing our selves as we reconstruct our visions of world communities entails deconstructing the stories we tell (of) ourselves and the desires that inform them. Angela McRobbie (1994) points to how such reassessment reaps important political possibilities:

> It is not so much a question of what is left behind, what fragments of the disassembled self can be picked up and put together again, but rather how might the continual process of putting oneself together be transformed to produce the empowerment of subordinate groups and social categories. This might mean living with fragmentation, with the reality of *inventing the self rather than endlessly searching for the self* (emphasis mine). (72)

While poststructural theories may de-center the subject, the importance of the subject as a central point of transformation is not lost but reinscribed with, I would argue, greater political potential. Herein is the project of poststructural auto/biography.

From this perspective, then, as Robert Graham (1991) points out, "the poststructural turn" need not entail a turn away from auto/biographical writing. Instead, this turn can lead us toward "a view of auto/biography in education as an intertextual and intersubjective project" (147) that aims to create the conditions by which "students come collectively to understand some of the workings of ideology and power and their relation to the construction of self and culture" (152). In this sense, there is no paradox in poststructural attention to auto/biography; instead, there is the commonality of purpose—beyond cliches of nature, essence, and universality—of discerning the workings of the social on the site of construction: the subject-body (see Chapter 2). This chapter explores such potential by elaborating on the poststructural project of auto/biography and its pedagogical challenges for both teachers and students.

■ The Allure of Auto/Biography

For those interested in the possibilities of auto/biography within a poststructural pedagogy, it is significant that the intensification of academic interest in narrative and auto/biography coincides with theories and educational philosophies that center the individual. This parallel development, however, is more than mere coincidence, for it also demonstrates how academic machinery and educational practices of modernism are complicit in enshrining a theory of self—the roots of which are found in the historical tracings of liberal humanism. That is, no theoretical version of self can be separate from questions of the vested interests attached to such versions: Whose interests and what ideologies are promoted and secured by a particular version of self? Narrative, the textual site of most claims to unity and coherence, and at the center of which is the unified subject/character, as a form, reflects the preferred notion of self and meaning in current circulation. Lack of political attention to such questions of narrative can be a political practice of hegemony; auto/biography, or auto/biographical writing, can be a particular personalization of the political practices of narrative.

However, what is noteworthy about the flurry of attention to auto/biography goes beyond this now well-established version of the relationship of knowledge practices and power. What increased attention to ideologies of individualism and autonomy more interestingly suggests is an anxiety over their continued dominance. The insurgence, in the form of political resistance, against the social order at the center of which has been the White, bourgeois, heterosexual male (the implied self of the liberal humanist tradition), threatens not only this order but also the forms of knowledge that hold it in place. Thus, unproblematic or romantic notions of the power of story and/or the educationally redemptive powers of auto/biography—even where applauded by those whose agendas might appear more radical[3]—must be approached cautiously, for notions are never innocent; they always participate in larger ideological constructs. What poststructural theories forewarn of is how, in any and every practice of auto/biography, there is the complicity of enclosure, even in the most conscious efforts at disclosure (Schenke 1991). The caveat holds: to tell one story is to silence others; to present one version of self is to withhold other versions of self.

In this respect, it is possible to locate part of the appeal, for many, of poststructural theories, in the reprieve it provides from the tyranny of discourses of the self supported through institutional doctrines founded in liberal humanism; that is, a release from the contradictions between dominant versions of the self and the lived realities of multiple selves negotiated within the confines of discourses of patriarchy, heterosexual imperative, White supremacy, and late capitalism. The attention to ambiguity, paradox, and difference—more complex and subtle renderings of experience—is libratory, in itself. To fail to connect these movements—the emphasis on narrative and the emergence of poststructural theories—would be foolhardy, for it also would be to fail to recognize what is at stake socially, culturally, politically, and educationally in versions of the self legitimized through public, popular, and institutional discourses (Graham 1991, 153).

In particular, members of socially marginalized groups have found in poststructural theories a means to theorize and name the workings of historical oppression and its relationship to the colonization of subjectivity. Ironically, attacks on the problematics of identity politics have also been fueled by poststructural theories that challenge the essentializing and homogenizing tendencies of any identity regulation (Gates, Jr. 1985; Miller 1991). This struggle, as pointed out by McRobbie in the preceding section, suggests the potential for exciting, if unsettling, collective- and self-reflections through poststructural approaches to pressing social problems. Yet, the contradiction aside, the shared point of the increased profile of poststructural theories and the insurgence of postcolonial[4] struggles is a struggle over the material and discursive grounds on which notions of self, identity, and representation are formed.

Many literary theorists have pointed to the political functions of narrative, in terms both of the version of self it assumes, enshrines, and reproduces (Belsey 1980) and the function of narrative in the structuring and channeling of desire. Dominant practices of auto/biography perform similar political functions as those traditionally assigned to narrative. The allure of auto/biography is, in part, then, the same as that of narrative: the illusion of the seamless web of experience, at the center of which is the (modernist) self coming into fuller rationality. Approaching auto/biography from a poststructural perspective entails challenging these conventions and the hegemonies they sustain while also using the texts of personal experience to further emancipatory projects. In part, this change of perspective entails addressing the desires— the urges toward unity and wholeness—out of which the allure of auto/ biography is secured—the present longings that propel its narrative lines.

The extent to which these desires are at the forefront of the popular psyche of North America may be seen in the upsurge of attention to films in which an overt personal narrative component is present. The overwhelming attention and praise given the film *Forrest Gump* is one example. Billed as "the story of a lifetime," of "an innocent at large in an America that is losing its innocence," Forrest is "the embodiment of an era" (video jacket). As Forrest sits at a bus stop, he narrates his story to whomever shares the bench with him. Riders come and go as Forrest's story unfolds in a blend of personal narrative and social history highlighted through the use of period television footage that places Forrest Ordinary-Everyman Gump at the heart of a largely unproblematized American history from the advent of the King, Elvis Presley, through various presidencies and assassinations, the Vietnam War, and the Reagan years. Forrest's story is a linear map; his (sense of) self, his identity, is unwavering and unconflicted. Gump's culture is a culture of simplifications. In this sense, his story is nostalgic, a requiem for modernity; and in its widespread appeal is a desire for the old order in which the United States occupies the center. *Forrest Gump* is certainly not the only marker of such nostalgia.[5] I here point to its production and appeal as, among other things, a symptom of a crisis in modernity in which versions of self and history—and accompanying notions of auto/biography—are high stakes across a wide range of cultural fronts. For educators, these points are not merely theoretical, for in the versions of self, meaning, and history promoted by any representation, and in those adopted pedagogically, are, too, the limits and possibilities of agency in the making of our own places in history—the situatedness to which auto/biography bears witness.

The oppositional stories of the past three decades—in particular, those stories forged out of postcolonial and feminist consciousnesses— have heightened an awareness of/and the extent to which versions of history openly compete in the public arena. In this sense the *power* of story has taken on a more radical dimension within the public consciousness.

The urge *to tell*, within such a context, becomes a moral imperative, a call to witness, as it were, the truths of the past.[6] What is important from a poststructural perspective is to interrogate the will to truth that informs these stories as we also celebrate their textual presence, what Arlene Schenke (1991) calls "the parodic moment of genealogy—the moment where subjugated knowledges are at once 'true,' but also 'made to be true' in light of political necessities and desires in the present" (54). This seeming contradiction is not ultimate anarchy, in which can be found no truth, but, rather, is reflective story, in which the truth effects of the partial story are also told: telling as social relation. Ignoring such complicities in auto/biographical writing goes beyond the failure to be reflexive. As Henry Giroux (1994) notes about the construction of popular memory, failure to confront the mediating conditions of representations of memory "runs the risk of reproducing a politics that is silent about its own pedagogical formation and thus [is] unresponsive to how it silences or terrorizes" (45). No less can be demanded of auto/biographical work in education than the ongoing self-reflexivity around pedagogical stories and the stories that are our pedagogies.

■ Teaching Selves

Among the auto/biographical work that focuses on teaching, and that is widely available to readers, one example stands out for its particular relevance to the discussions of this chapter. My choice of the memoir, *French Lessons*, by Alice Kaplan, rests on its explicit attention to my concerns here: the construction of identity as multifaceted inflictions of desire for/and memory, knowledge, and cultural place. Further, it is the memoir of a teacher, a Duke University professor of French literature, who uses her considerable skills to confront the investments of her own claims to knowledge and pedagogy as she mines the memories on which they were formed. As such, Kaplan demonstrates what I claim is the central importance of auto/biography *in* education: the contradictory and telltale signs of how, and for what, knowledge/education—literacy—come to matter.

The desire that informs this choice, however, reveals more intimate connections. My most recent auto/biographical writing attempted to connect fiction, theories of political economy, reading, culture and pedagogy, and subjectivity as a means to articulate a project of social transformation that rested on the contradictory politics of identity and cultural/geographical place (Kelly 1993). I chose as the focus of my writing the emergence of a specific and conflicted cultural identity within the multi-textual dimensions of schooling, culture, and place. At one point in that piece, I wrote:

> As a female child in a small Newfoundland community, school was a place where I was subjected to history, knowledge, language and culture as imperialism. I absorbed residue curriculum and instruction from an English (British) system of schooling as indifference, belittlement, homogenization, and service to God, nation and men. That, according to some of its terms, I succeeded so well in this system horrifies me now as I contend with my own losses and disruptures. Whose language do I speak? To what community do I belong? What culture speaks for me? In what history might I be found? (57–8)

I was drawn to Kaplan's book because it addresses the issue of knowledge as masquerade—French language and culture as "a place to hide," (216)—in a very different way than I, and, by confronting conscious complicity, with a greater attention than I to the subtleties of the dialectic between cultural imposition and (chosen?) acquisition. My reading of Kaplan thus allowed me to find another auto/biographical story (to which I will refer further in a later section of this chapter) and it was/is the desire for this (my) story that was my first impulse toward her book.[7]

In her memoir, Kaplan, a Jewish American who grew up in Minneapolis, traces, from childhood to her time of writing, her fascination with and attraction to French language and culture. The memoir focuses Kaplan's experiences through her study of French, her research on the literature of French fascism and her teaching of French language and literature. In particular, Kaplan addresses the impact of the absence of her father—a lawyer at the Nuremberg trials, who died just two days before her eighth birthday—on her desire to perfect the French language, to surround herself with French culture, and to make a career of teaching French literature.

At one point in this poignantly clear and insightful memoir, Kaplan recalls one of her teachers, the deconstructionist Paul de Man, and the impact on her of the posthumous revelation that de Man had been a Nazi collaborator, and had written pro-Nazi and anti-Semitic articles as part of his assignment with a Belgian newspaper during the war. In this particular reflection, Kaplan bemoans the intellectual loss de Man's failure to expose his past bequeathed on his students.[8] Wishing to avoid similar failures in her own relationships with students, at the end of the reflection Kaplan asks, "How do I tell [students] who I am, why I read the way I do? What do students need to know about their teachers?" (174). In this section, I will use Kaplan's questions—and her memoir—as the basis of an analysis of the complexities of auto/biography within a pedagogy of desire.

In her initial questions, Kaplan addresses her own desire to have her students know her as their teacher, a desire that comes, at least in part, out of Kaplan's own experience of de Man's failure of her desires in their student-teacher relationship. Yet, the tone of these questions suggests a yearning for something prior to the possibility of having others—in this case, students—know her; it bespeaks a longing to know herself and to be able to discern the relationship of her reading practices to that self. It is this prior longing, the fulfillment of which albeit is never fully accomplishable—what Joanne Pagano (1990) calls "the unslakeable desire to be known" (73)—that brings a radical sense to the questions Kaplan raises. This dilemma of self-knowing (a postmodern oxymoron) is caught by Kaplan elsewhere in her memoir when she refers to her "old struggle with teachers, wanting to know more about them than they knew about themselves" (171). However, having learned through her own experiences of schooling, from a teacher of literature, that "[w]riting is the opposite of making something present. . . . Writing is effacement" (75) and, from de Man, that auto/biography is "an impossible genre . . . where the more you try to confess, the more you lie" (173), she brings us, paradoxically enough, not only face-to-face with the limits of language as a means to erase the lack that is this desire to tell but, also, with the necessity of proceeding, nevertheless, with the fiction of telling.

One of the finest accomplishments of Kaplan's memoir is in how it heightens the deep and sometimes dark connections between the desire to teach others as part of a larger complex of desire, the making of the subject of embodied experience through the desires the history of our experiences break, mould, and carry into the present. In this sense, Kaplan's memoir is an exemplary and politically useful answer to her own initial questions. That is to say, Kaplan's memoir is not only about pedagogy, but it is also pedagogical, in that a reading of it can propel the process of reflection that addresses how it is that the life of a teacher is cast interminably within teaching practices: how we are and who we are when we teach. Addressing the question of the *need* for certain knowledge, in Kaplan's case, her need for French, she "airs her suspicions, her anger, her longings" (216) and in so doing constructs a model of discursive placement in which it is possible to see the meanings of lives as made of the specific social, cultural, and historical urgings that comprise *locatedness*. Prying at the discursive threads of these urgings, Kaplan's work insists that to question how the desire to learn, and what one desires to learn, remain lodged in the practices of teaching is a fundamental departing point for a self-conscious pedagogy.

In many respects, then, Kaplan answers her own questions, the initial pair ("[h]ow do I tell [students] who I am, why I read the way I do?") by *how* she accomplishes her memoir, and the final one ("[w]hat do students need to know about their teachers?") by *what* she accomplishes in it. However, she also realizes the implications of her inclination "to wrap things up too neatly in words" (216), the niggling insight that "every human knowledge has its own unconscious. . . . [E]very insight is inhabited by its own blindness" (Felman 1993, 71). Teachers need to examine not only the political character of our knowing but, as well, the politics of coming to know what it is teachers know. Kaplan's questions, by forging a direct relationship among desire ("[h]ow do I tell [students] . . . "), subjectivity (" . . . who I am . . . "), knowledge, and power (" . . . why I read the way I do?"), pinpoint the radical questions of pedagogy and, simultaneously, stress the inscription of these very questions within the lives of teachers. Stories that enclose—as they disclose—the dynamics of the vested interests of teachers in particular modes of knowledge production bear witness to the making and remaking of desire in the classroom. Students need to know that this is the case, both for their teachers and themselves. In short, students need to know the relationship of desire, knowledge and pedagogy so that they may be knowing participants in schooling (see Chapter 7). And students need to know this relationship for and of themselves as well as of those positioned as their teachers. By galvanizing such claims, Kaplan suggests the possibilities of auto/biography to demonstrate how desire, knowledge, schooling, and identity are complexly interconnected and how the social practices of education derive from and inevitably return to the landscape of subjectivity.

■ Reshaping Auto/Biographical Practice

[A]t times I think through autobiography: that is to say, the chain of associations that I am pursuing in my reading passes through things that happened to me.

—Jane Gallop (1988, 4)

In this section, I question the practice of auto/biography through my experiences of preparation of a teaching unit called "Looking

Auto/Biographically." My focus is the specific experience of preparation, for it was there that the auto/biographical moment to which I will
attend coalesced into insights about proceeding pedagogically through
auto/biography. What follows, then, is an instance of writing pedagogy
auto/biographically or, at least, of preparing pedagogy auto/biographi-
cally. My foremost concern, in concert with Gallop, is to show how
what I was attempting to teach—the theoretical questions I wished to
raise—"passed through things that happened to me" and how, in so
doing, confronted me with challenges for proceeding auto/biographi-
cally in a poststructural-informed pedagogy.

In this particular teaching unit, part of a course entitled "Literacy,
Cultural Politics and Identity," the class would choose photographs as
a beginning point for writing auto/biographically. There exist many
examples of the pedagogical use of photography, with or without
accompanying writing (Buckingham and Sefton-Greene 1994; Taylor
1993) that suggest the potential of this "dual-media" approach. My plan
was that each student who chose to complete the exercise (one option
among many) would choose two pictures from a childhood collection;
a third picture would be taken in the present, its focus a suggestion of
auto/biographical meaning—a deliberate and conscious construct—
from the vantage point of the present (as opposed to a memory constructed from the same vantage point using traces from the past). I
would demonstrate a version of the exercise using my own pictures,
framing the discussion around the notion that

> photographs (ordinary, everyday, everyone's snaps) are *mis*-used.
> They are seen as evidence, traces, proofs, in a word—answers. I
> think that we have to see them as questions: they pose questions
> for us. (Corrigan 1983/4, 29)

The questions that arose from the photographs would form the basis of
a piece of auto/biographical writing around critical memory. The individual exercises would be followed by voluntary sharing and extended
work among those who had completed the photo installment exercise as
one step to promote "new forms of subjectivity via a refusal of individ-
uality and a diffusion of the sites and practices from which domination
can be challenged" (Lather 1991, 96). The exercise was designed to
demonstrate, inter-textually, how both photography and auto/biogra-
phy, as cultural productions, are highly and deliberately selective, are
discursively and ideologically bound, and rely on absence and omission
as well as—and as importantly as—inclusion. As Rosalind Coward
(1985) reminds us, "the mirror with a memory" was the slogan attached

to the first photographic processes, that of Louis Daguerre in the 1840s (49). The notion of making and preserving memories continues to be a dominant characterization of the marketing of contemporary popular photography. From this exercise, we could make problematic the notion of memory, inscription and meaning while also addressing the many texts out of which auto/biography and subjectivity are constituted. But, as this section shall demonstrate, getting there is, at least, half of this teacher's story.

Every Picture Tells a Story[9]

The childhood pictures I chose to introduce these notions to the class have always fascinated me (see Figures 3.1 and 3.2). This fascination, a form of perpetual questioning/wondering, was a major reason for my choices. Together, these two pictures exemplify a pattern that emerges in my childhood photos: memorable moments of cross-dressing, my "dressing up"—in whatever gendered "disguise"—as a photographic occasion, an "event" to be marked and recorded. In this way, then, my childhood photos can be construed as "evidence" of a contest for (my) gendered identity. The third picture (see Figure 3.3) was taken specifically for the exercise I have outlined above. It was designed to represent some of the ways I "picture" myself, some of the questions I ask (of) myself, in my work as a woman academic. Together, they form a photomontage, the point from which I begin my inquiry.

Figure 3.1

Figure 3.2

Figure 3.3

What follows are questions: of theory and reading; of readings of theory; of theories of reading. Yet, I shall call these questions stories; I shall call these stories auto/biography; and I shall also call these auto/biographies fragments—of desire—manifested (man-infested?) through "looking auto/biographically" while proceeding theoretically. Their purchase is in partial answers that are also further questions. In the sense that auto/biography can "sneak up on you," these fragments are also, in some ways, "accidents." These accidents are presented as open, "writerly" (Barthes 1979) texts that refuse their assumed status as evidence and, instead, resume the status of *provocateur*, that which provokes (further) questions as suggestions of efforts to show some ways in which theory "passes through things that happened to me."

Fragment One

As the effects of a subtle and politically enforced performativity, gender is an "act," as it were, that is open to splittings, self-parody, self-criticism, and those hyperbolic exhibitions of "the natural" that, in their very exaggeration, reveal its fundamentally phantasmatic status.

—Judith Butler (1990, 146–7)

In her discussion of impersonation, Jane Gallop (1995) argues for a notion of "the personal as mask . . . as performance, as what one takes on": *im-personation*—"*appearing as a person*" (9). *Im-personation* is always gendered, so that there is always a sense in which "being any gender is a drag" (Bryson and de Castell 1995, 24). How can this *double entendre* be "read off" the dueling desires of the childhood photos (Figures 3.1 and 3.2): the Catholic schoolgirl child-of-God, the virgin bride suggested by the Roman Catholic sacrament of First Holy Communion; and the emerging tomboy, the inscription for the girl who refused to be one. My childhood photos are marked by numerous examples of such cross-dressing. Precisely what and whose desires and fantasies inform these events and urge their record? How are these (contradictory and contrary) desires carried forward as traces (of complicity in the desires of others) in the woman academic (Figure 3.3): "what precisely is masked by masquerade" (Butler 1990, 47)?

Fragment Two

Why do people want to adopt another culture? Because there's something in their own they don't like, that doesn't name them.

—Alice Kaplan (1993, 209)

What I learned in school was that successful forms of self-violation are
rewarded with credentials. . . .

—Magda Lewis (1993, 193)

Kaplan's memoir can be read as a convincing analysis of and argument for living in drag, *in absentia*. In the excerpt of an earlier auto/bio-
graphical piece, quoted in a previous section of this chapter, I raise the
question of schooling as the imposition of (still more) cultural drag.
The circumstances of my *im-personation* are such that I am less content
than Kaplan to "live in exile from myself" (210) and more suspect of the
conditions of power that surrounded my decisions. In an ongoing
struggle with cultural (dis)placement, I question the formative circumstances of "my contradictory desires—to be home where I was not
(entirely) at home; to be away that I might be more at home with
myself" (Kelly 1993, 60). What desires—or what desired identities—
fueled "the self-embraced project of my education" (Lewis 1993, 188),
the route to this alienation, this place/displacement? When, if ever, is
identity not a drag? What "goes missing" in masquerade?

Fragment Three

The struggle both to perform academically and to perform as feminine
must seem at times almost impossible. No wonder some of us split them
apart in various ways, or have different conscious and unconscious
methods for dealing with the unbearable contradictions.

—Valerie Walkerdine (1990, 144)

What is the position of the woman who identifies with men who identify
with women?

—Jane Gallop (1988, 100)

How is auto/biography infused with such splits? How is it possible
to conceive of auto/biography that resists an erasure of the splits? In
what ways is it possible to capture what may feel and be remembered as
"an assemblage of dark voids and unbridgeable gaps" (Shields 1993,
76)? How is an inclination toward auto/biography a practice of mediation and remediation, revisiting and revising, propelled by an ever-pre-
sent desire for wholeness and healing? How might an interrogation of
the urge of auto/biography (which shares some things with the urge of
photography)—"the idea that we can have control over our loss by
knowing the truth" (Walkerdine 1990, 101)—become a pedagogically

viable project? How have I betrayed this urge of auto/biography in my own photo selections (Figures 3.1, 3.2, and 3.3)? How have I resisted these urges by my refusal, here, of auto/biography, what some might call my shelter in the closet of theory?

The questions that arose from my preparation of "Looking Auto/Biographically" will form the basis of the auto/biographical "take"—the story—that I will share with my class. As such, the preparation shifted significantly my sense of the project at hand. What I initially conceived as a project around discourse, text, and subjectivity ("these are my meanings; these are the ways and means through which they have been shaped") became more acutely focused on issues of *desire* and subjectivity ("what *more* do I need to know; what auto/biographical absences do these pictures present?). Herein, and suddenly, with these questions, memory seemed indistinguishable from longing, identity and masquerade posed as one, and "a room of my own" became a partially lit closet. Auto/biography is unsettling work. Much more than "getting personal" (Miller 1991) or "getting there" (Schenke 1991), it is unpacking the sedimented layers of subjectivity through difficult questions, uncertain procedures, and irresolute findings.

As Kaplan demonstrates through *French Lessons*, much more must be said of *the pedagogue-as-auto/biographer* in the discussions of education and auto/biography. Ultimately, the projects we so enthusiastically shape for our students' engagements are, first and foremost, engaged by us as teachers. Confronted initially in the confines of the less revealing spaces of private offices and homes, the questions of who I am, why I read and teach the way I do, and what I know and do not (yet) know of my auto/biography no less impede and propel my more public pedagogy. The answers to these questions are always historically contingent, a maneuvre of competing desires and relations of power. Contextualized as such, auto/biography is always both disclosure and enclosure, both effacement and revelation, both impossible and necessary. These conditions of auto/biographical practice must be its pedagogical starting points: What precedes the story, the *coming to story*, strikes me as an active dynamic of a self-reflective pedagogy.

■ The Lives Texts Tell

[A]utobiography is constructed as narrative and not as unmediated self-reflection, and . . . the discourse of the genre is part of contemporary ideological constructions of the self. Uncovering and investigating both the generic and social processes of this construction marks the beginnings of a politically useful knowledge, a conceptualized "making strange" of what appears to be natural and universal—the self.

—Bennison and Porteous (1989, 176-7)

Our identities as subjects are not tied to or dependent upon some transcendental regime of truth beyond the territory of the profane and the mundane. Rather, they are constitutive of the literacies we have at our disposal through which we make sense of our day-to-day politics of living.

—Lankshear and McLaren (1993, 386)

The question of *what do students need to know?* must be asked when students are the subjects of the question, that is, when, as a student, one asks, *what is it I need to know about myself?* and, then, *what desires have shaped this present knowing?* As I have indicated in the previous section, for teachers—and students of teacher education—another question follows: *How do I carry these desires into my relationships with students through my pedagogies?* However, teachers continually invoke assumptions and decisions about what it is students need to know. Joanne Pagano (1990) notes:

When we teach we mean to change people. We mean to bring them to new ways of encountering and constructing the world. But we must remember always that the end educational project is *their* world, too. One of the greatest temptations for teachers is to colonize their students' consciousness. Education should bring people to the place from which they can go on alone and make up their own stories. (202)

Working the dialectic between what teachers feel students should know and what students might (come to) feel they need to know has been a pivotal point in my own teaching.[10] Ensuring that students have an opportunity to confront questions of their own constituted relationship of knowledge, desire, and pedagogy becomes an important moment in maintaining this dialectic.

As one aspect of establishing the conditions of such interrogation, auto/biography is one option through which students may explore how an engagement of the multiple texts of the course regulate—that is, expand and/or limit—the possibilities of their own auto/biographies. In short, the assignment takes seriously the poststructural claim that all "classroom practice is ultimately linked to theories of the subject, the social, learning and teaching" (Luke and Gore 1992, 193), which find their impact first and foremost in the personal. Proceeding from this claim, auto/biography becomes a site of struggle, the place from which lives tell of the shaping of dreams and desires through the discourses and practices of schooling. For example, in "Literacy, Cultural Politics, and Identity," students may choose to construct a literacy log through which they trace the textual density and variety of personal and professional literacies, and the discourses that govern them, as contextualized social practices.

There are two problems, in particular, that can accompany such an endeavor and that are part of the underbelly of the allure of auto/biography to which I have earlier referred: transference and scopophilia. Madeleine Grumet (1991) points to the problem of auto/biography when it takes the form of the single story: "When there is one story, it becomes *the* story, *my* story, and when it is delivered to another, it arrives gift-wrapped in transference" (72). Auto/biography in education has been haunted by the scepter of "the one presumed to know," who claims, in relation to the auto/biography and its narrator, the position of the one who *assumes* to know. In such practices, imposition can replace self-reflexivity; transference, rather than being deflected, is galvanized, a situation that can create a pedagogical relationship of dependency in which the student is most vulnerable and in which the teacher maintains editorial control. Because women's stories are often testimonies to trauma, transference positions the teacher as a therapist within "the analytic dyad" (Grumet 1991, 76). The importance of the well-established insights of "the implication of psychoanalysis in pedagogy and of pedagogy in psychoanalysis" (Felman 1987, 75) and the extent to which the former implication has *not* been taken up in teacher education together suggest the shaky ground on which both teacher and student, differently, can here find themselves.

Scopophilia, a fondness for unreciprocated looking—voyeurism—marks many pedagogical practices of auto/biography.[11] Yet, this aspect of auto/biographical practices in education is rarely addressed. The assumption of authority—the *power* to look—can blind us to the imposition of auto/biography as an aspect of pedagogy. Not all students want to participate, actively and openly, in auto/biographical writing. Many may not wish to address their auto/biography to the teacher. Many may feel auto/biography is unimportant, a cultural imposition or an unhelpful exercise in narcissism. Such concerns arise out of an ambivalence about the impact of looking, especially if mutuality is absent from the pedagogical practice of auto/biography.

This story may demonstrate my point. A student once submitted to me, as part of the requirements of the course in which she was enrolled, an elaborate and photo-accompanied auto/biography she entitled "A Pack of Lies." I am certain her stories were not lies, certainly not in the usual sense of the word; but her choice of title served to remind me of the ambiguity and risk that constitute the practice of auto/biography and the ambivalence that can mark the act of submission—subjecting a story to some *other's* gaze. The title was especially well chosen, for it positioned me, as the reader, to adopt an ambivalent posture toward the assignment. Positioning me in this way also created a space for the student—a more secure space, in some respects—to speak her stories. How she negotiated her contradictory desires to tell and to conceal was less about her selection of stories, or the details of those stories, and more about her positioning of the reader within them. The title also represented an appropriately ironic stance around the work of auto/ biography. The potential depoliticizing effect of such positioning, however, poses yet another problem symptomatic of many postmodern turns in social commentary.

Exoticization and appropriation are also potential problems of work with/in auto/biography. Both exoticization and appropriation are practices of power, the bases of which are similar to those of scopophilia. Exoticization—practices that simultaneously enhance allure *and* difference, creating an "attractive strangeness"—is a process whereby difference is constituted in the interests and through the fantasies of the dominant (hooks 1992; Walkerdine, 1990). Appropriation occurs through practices in which the culture, identities, and representations of marginalized groups are consumed—viewed, interpreted, and reiterated (re-presented)—through the lenses, on the terms, and in the interests of the dominant (Ellsworth 1992). The expectation to do auto/ biography and the practice of auto/biography itself within an educational setting where an auto/biography is addressed (or at least submitted) to an other allows for the possibility of both exoticization and appropriation. Again, these potential problems are not an argument against auto/biographical work but one for reflexive telling and reading.

As Grumet (1991) points out, multiple narratives (retellings) and multiple interpreters (rereadings) are important components in challenging dominant notions of auto/biography while also supplanting the authoritative gaze of the teacher. Resisting closure and encouraging a vision of the collective, as well as the personal, struggles that are borne out in auto/biography are ongoing challenges to effective radical pedagogy. Yet, it is here that poststructural theories are most helpful. A notion of auto/biography as readings of selves positioned within a larger textuality insists that this larger textuality be interrogated for ways in which we read and are (culturally) read to, for the ways in which we have learned to look and the ways in which we are looked at. In other words, auto/biography demands an investigation of our *becoming in*, and our *coming to*, literacy, to assimilated (and often assimilationist) readings of the textual world and the word. Such an approach to auto/biography *decenters* the subject, focusing attention, instead, on how the subject is constituted within a dynamics of power across a wide array of textual and discursive practices.

While such an educational focus does not necessarily diminish the intimacy of auto/biography, it does enhance the sociality of self; as well, it can challenge the ideology of individualism, the generic (and genre) practices of narrative, and the educational presumptions that can surround "doing auto/biography." Neither does such an approach constitute a rejection of the possibility of truth. As Alice Kaplan (1993) notes, "[t]here are truths about the past but there is no authority, no policeman, ready and able to pin them down" (213). Truth is multiple—and always ever partial. Unsettled notions of what constitutes the personal, self, memory, history, and truth do, however, create the grounds for a more critical and reflective auto/biographical practice.

■

Delving into auto/biographical work, in particular through a focus on the textual density of literate lives, invariably reveals the impact of the popular in the negotiation of meanings of self and community. In the two chapters that follow, I address dimensions of the engagement of the popular within postmodern culture and its pedagogical effects at the level of the subject of the popular. Of concern in both chapter 4 and chapter 5 are ways of engaging readings of the popular as pedagogical texts, starting points in the (re)constitution of social identities and partial insights into the terminable question of *what it is that students (and teachers) need to know.*

Four

INCESSANT CULTURE

The Promise of the Popular

■ In educational work with students in auto/biography of the sort outlined in the previous chapter, one theme emerges consistently: engagements with popular culture are among the most creative and persuasive influences on personal and collective identity. Powerfully and repeatedly demonstrated within auto/biographical stories of literacy are the ways in which "discourses of the popular become discourses of ourselves" (C. Luke 1993, 176). Within traditional literacy education practices, however, little attention has been given the constitutive effects of popular culture[1] beyond cliched, reactionary, and combative commentary designed to maintain the indefensible modernist cultural divides of high (discriminating) and low (popular) cultural practices. The stubborn classism demonstrated in such commentary ignores, as it simultaneously fails to understand fully, the complex political relationship of culture and desire.

It is even more disheartening that this classism has persisted and even deepened alongside and within other apparently progressive movements. The "hostility to mass culture" (Giroux 1990, 19) demonstrated in modernist ideals, theories, and practices, and that informs some forms of feminisms, critical social theories, and radical pedagogies, has been a major obstacle in the engagement of transformative social projects. The antagonisms toward the popular are also part of the rejection of so-called undisciplined pleasures and desires as disruptive and threatening to bourgeois moral order (Walkerdine 1990). In the sense in which Emma Goldman said it best—"If I can't dance, I don't want to be part of your revolution"—the anti-libidinous character of some progressive discourses positions many to feel a choice between pleasure and politics must exist. What such positioning accomplishes, aside from the likely rejection of politics rather than pleasure, is the denial of the complex and contradictory character of engagements with the popular. The popular is a site of problematic pleasures, but it is also a site of pleasurable politics, a place where hopeful resistance, longings, and possibilities are represented.

It is precisely this recognition of the promise as well as the problematics of the popular that has resulted in two decades of concerted attention to popular culture in an emerging field known as cultural studies. Within cultural studies, all social practices are approached to discern the work they do on the subject (Johnson 1983). Within the postmodern, where the proliferating "image is everything," the interactive effects of representation, power, and desire, at the level of subject formation, become more politically pressing. Modes of subjectivity, forms of representation, identity politics, and cultural practices take precedence in a culturally colonized global ethos in which the political stakes of difference and for Others are high.

In a world drastically altered by extensive global interaction, hyper-communications, and rapid information production, the postmodern is marked by a series of cultural shifts. Within the postmodern, virtual reality supplants reality; the imitation supplants the original; multiple, relative (not relational) truths supplant universal truth; nomadic existence and border-crossing supplant rootedness in place and culture; morphing and drag supplant stable identity; specific stories of chaos, contradiction, and struggle supplant grand narratives of progress, religion, and civilization; and difference supplants homogeneity. Within the postmodern, parody, irony, and self-referentiality provide the most telling social commentary in which nothing is sacred, nothing is permanent. The postmodern condition is one of both peril and possibility. While postmodern theory may, as yet, be largely contained within academic institutions, its practical face is highly prevalent in popular culture and media. In all its guises, it challenges and deconstructs the foundations on which the modern world was structured.

It is impossible to address popular culture without understanding the premises of postmodernism, for it is through the popular that the postmodern condition is culturally expressed and reproduced. While this account of postmodern culture may sound despairing, what I am most concerned to present is the sense of possibility that it provides for literacy education.[2] Here, I draw on the distinction made by Teresa Ebert (1991) between ludic and resistance postmodernisms. As Ebert notes, there are

> two radically different notions of politics in postmodernism. Ludic politics is a textual practice that seeks open access to the free play of signification in order to disassemble the dominant cultural policy (totality), which tries to restrict and stabilize meaning. Whereas resistance postmodernism . . . insists on a materialist political practice that works for equal access of all to social resources and for an end to the exploitive exercise of power. (887)

The possibility of postmodernism for literacy education lies, then, in the destabilization of meaning for emancipatory purposes. The *relational* rather than relative basis of meaning, its contexts, and politics, becomes the defining difference of resistance postmodernism and literacy education.

This chapter proceeds beyond the modernist, classist strictures of debates about the popular, toward an examination of the promise of the popular within the postmodern, the hope on which incessant culture insists. Cultural studies, with its focus on the representational and relational (Roman and Christian-Smith 1988) character of a wide range of cultural forms, I argue, provides the means toward important insights for renewed and expanded directions in literacy education in a postmodern age. The directive question in this relationship is how cultural practices of representation and meaning court desires and mobilize identities: in other words, are pedagogical. Of particular importance in addressing this question is the cultural work of the popular, the site on which dominant habits of desire are circulated, reiterated, and challenged.

■ **Cultural Studies and Popular Desires**

> [I]n its production of meanings, affective investments, even ways of life,
> mass culture may be seen as a primary point at which the public meets
> the private, politics meets pleasure, and pedagogy meets the personal—
> the point at which, as it is taken up by interlocking systems of exchange
> (textual, affective, discursive and commodity), desire itself is disciplined
> and educated.
>
> —Lynne Joyrich (1995, 49)

In the past two decades, research that explores the relationship of culture and power has pointed to the ways in which *culture works* in the constitutive processes of subject/identity formation and social relations. Literacy educators at all levels and on all sites have begun to apply the methods of analysis of cultural studies to forge more insightful and democratic literacy practices. These efforts are propelled by two specific urges: to refute the entrenched elitism of dominant literacy practices; and to develop the student or reader of culture, a necessary educational objective in the postmodern age (Buckingham and Sefton-Green 1994; Christian-Smith 1993; Morgan 1993; Gilbert and Taylor 1991; Hilton 1996; Giroux 1994). A large part of a cultural studies approach to literacy education entails examining how literacy practices are implicated in, carry forward, and actively constitute particular social desires and anxieties as forms of social regulation. The political project of "cultural studies in the service of critical literacy" (Berlin 1993, 261), one discursive model of critical literacy (see Chapter 1), and the focus of this chapter, is to constitute reflective, agenic readers of culture whose modes of participation as literate citizens enable social change.

Educators interested in recognizing and developing multiple and critical literacies often look to media studies, the predominant focus of which is techniques, ideologies, and effects of media. A fundamental, although often unstated, premise of media studies is that if media toxify then media literacy is a detoxifier. Much of the emphasis in media studies is on the effects of the technology; the reader is situated as the largely passive receptor of its messages. It is often the case in such discourses of media studies that little attention is given the affective investments of readers in media. In this respect, the shift from an emphasis on media to one on culture is more than semantic. If media often suggests an emphasis on technologies and their effects, culture emphasizes, or at least has the potential to emphasize, the lived engagements of media and meaning through how desires, dreams, identities, and social

relations are shaped—for culture is the site on which these are represented and reiterated. This point of engagement is where cultural studies can, should, does, and must continue to distinguish itself from media
studies.

Investigating and analyzing the workings of culture as social practices requires a reconceptualization of meaning-making: text, reader,
readings, and context are redefined and reinscribed (see chapter 1).
David Buckingham and Julian Sefton-Green (1994) articulate some of
the more pointed differences that accompany such a shift in focus.
Their approach, which they loosely describe as a cultural studies one
based on questions of engagement and use, necessitates a

> [m]ove beyond the familiar notion of reading as an isolated
> encounter between reader and text . . . [and a] look not so much
> at the relation between the reader and the text as at the ways in
> which meanings and tastes are socially established and circulated.
> Rather than merely concentrating on how young people read
> particular texts, we also want to consider the *social functions* that
> their readings perform. Broadly speaking, we want to move away
> from a notion of reading as merely a matter of individual
> "response," and to redefine it as part of a broader process of
> social circulation and use, which we might term "culture." (18)

In short, an examination of the intersections of culture and power such
as that advocated by Buckingham and Sefton-Green would focus on
how "texts are often taken up as part of a broader attempt to analyze
how individuals and social identities are mobilized, engaged, and transformed within circuits of power informed by issues of race, gender,
class, ethnicity and other social formations" (Giroux 1994, 129). Such a
focus on circuits of power and/in culture also brings cultural studies in
line with the objectives of critical literacy (see chapter 1) through attention to feminist and postcolonial politics of identity, desire, and difference (hooks 1992; Dyson 1993; Luke 1994).

In the shift towards cultural studies, several interrelated emphases
can be articulated. A key word is *engagement*. How are discourses
engaged, negotiated, and transformed by the subjects that they attempt
to position? What meanings are created and reiterated through engagement, and with what effects? How do readers negotiate the contradictory terrain of culture and identity through *engagement with* media?
A key focus of engagement is *affective investment* as the "tie that binds"
culture and identity. What desires propel particular engagements?
What promises of pleasure, what rewards for desire, are accrued

through forms of engagement? What emotional gains are weighted against and with what political urges? How is the subject affectively constructed, that is, how is the structuring of desire an ongoing cultural project of the subject?

The project that propels such questions is a discernment of the *political terms of engagement*. In this sense, culture is not static; rather, it is vital, negotiable, and often contradictory (see Chapter 1). This point is crucial to understanding how social inequities are embedded, naturalized, but also challenged in and through our everyday cultural lives. Such emphatic questions reveal the ways in which classism, racism, sexism, heterosexism, and other social dis-orders are the consequences of desires constructed on the foundations of social inequities (see Chapter 5). How else is it possible to explain how so many find pleasure in that which fundamentally denies aspects of our and others' beings?

The price of engaging our pleasures is never separate from the social cost of disordered dreams. Race is a political category, not an essential difference; middle-class values are learned, not bred; heterosexuality is common, not normal. If it is our structured desires—structured in and through culture—and our folly in how we pursue them that has resulted in the creation of a world in which, for many, it is difficult to realistically invest hopes, it is the responsibility of all cultural workers to reconfigure the cultural landscape. The source and effect of our folly can be found in culture; but there, also, can be found a source of hope. The structuring of our desires, dreams, and fantasies begins upon entry into the social world; culture is the series of practices and processes by which dreams, desires, and fantasies are reiterated and/or restructured and reformulated. As much cultural studies research has pointed out (Gilbert and Taylor 1991; Walkerdine 1990; Radway 1986), fantasy and reality are not separate. Rather, the two are deeply intertwined, the former actively structuring how we attempt to live out and give meaning to the latter.

Cultural studies concerns itself with looking at how any medium is implicated in such ongoing psychic and social processes of culture. Herein, any cultural practice—advertisements, dance, popular reading, internet dialoguing—is located within its layers of cultural meaning and is read as meaning-full. Such reading requires moving beyond clichéd and/or monolithic readings of culture. It also involves finding the points of resistance where culture questions itself as it also proceeds oppressively. For example, moving beyond clichéd readings of culture might enable us to read dance as more than sexualized leisure, popular reading as more than trashy material in the hands of the culturally unsophisticated, and network dialoguing as more than a threat to cultural order.

If we see cultural practices as *political*, that is, steeped in social relations of power related, for example, to social class, gender, race, sexual practice, etc., and, further, as sites of *possibility*, as practices that have socially transformative potential, other readings than the dominant ones become available. For those who embrace it, popular culture is primarily about pleasure, but it is also and often about resistance, albeit oftentimes expressed in ineffective ways. Through these lenses of pleasure *and* resistance, dance becomes also a practice of exploding the boundaries set by the daily regulating and disciplining of the body (Gotfrit 1991; McRobbie 1994); popular reading, i.e., romance reading, becomes a site on which heterosexual women take "time out" from the disappointments and broken dreams oftentimes lived within patriarchal relations (Radway 1986; Willinsky and Hunniford 1993); and internet browsing becomes a way of defining one's own reading and writing *for connection* to real others with common interests. In other words, each of these practices is in some ways a site of resistance to some aspect of the present social order, and each demonstrates the fundamental yet often missed point that "social agency is employed in the activation of *all* meanings" (McRobbie 1994, 23). Yet it is difficult to see these hopeful urges, these agenic impulses, if one is simply dismissive of the popular. To focus on the possibility of the popular, however, is not to valorize it. Rather, the popular must be seen as a site of contradictory practices, the complexities of which pose possibility and promise as well as entrapment.

Cultural studies is a broad, diverse, and interdisciplinary field of practice, the multiple directions of which have been mapped out by several theorists.[3] Yet its main objective is quite consistent: "to map the tangle of a particular cultural practice" (Morgan 1993, 110) through the investigation of the multiple sites on which, and the contradictory ways in which, a specific cultural practice is formed, informed, invented, and reinvented. Angela McRobbie (1994) captures well the thrust of the analytic method of cultural studies in an increasingly complexified cultural world as the

> examining of all those processes which accompany the production of meaning in culture, not just the end-product: from where it is socially constructed to where it is socially deconstructed and contested, in the institutions, practices and relationships of everyday life around us. (41)

From this perspective, the various aspects of the contexts and practices of production, public-ation, distribution, marketing, and audience engagement are examined as informing the spiraling work of culture: persuasions of meaning. By locating the nexus of culture and politics in the structuring of desire and identity, cultural studies provides significant insights into the pedagogies of persuasion and the persuasions of pedagogy.[4]

■ A Curriculum Example

In many Western countries, more progressive curriculum change related to language, literacy and culture has pointed to the necessity of addressing the notions of text and reading in broader conceptual terms. These shifts usually entail a movement beyond the more literal meanings of text-as-print and reading as print-engagement to more metaphorical ones in which text is a more broadly based and less rigidly bound cultural site and reading is the meaningful engagement of such polymorphous and fluid sites by an active meaning-making reader.[5] These shifts are noteworthy not only because they signal changes in the sphere of concern designated to a curriculum subject but also because underlying them are assumptions about the interrelationship of schooling, literacy, and culture that require examination. It is often the case that apparently expanding educational frameworks are often problematic precisely because they ignore or deny their own contracting tendencies.

In terms of such changes, and of interest here, is the extent to which the concerns of cultural studies are conceptualized and shaped as curriculum directions. Drawing on the notion of curriculum as cultural politics (see Chapter 1), it is possible to examine curriculum change as discursive in(ter)vention, as a reshaping of priorities and interests that is not innocent or apolitical. The example that follows is intended to point to what are emerging as fairly common contradictions within curriculum change, a consequence of efforts to manage an increasing number of counter-discourses of literacy, language, and culture. This curriculum example points to disquieting problems that can emerge when a force with which to be contended—popular culture—is rendered part of the zone of literacy curriculum.

In Canada, where provinces and territories have traditionally defined their own curriculum separate from, although rarely unrelated to, one another, several initiatives toward a common national curriculum and/or regional curriculum have been developed. In the Atlantic

Provinces, Canada's most easterly grouping of provinces, initiatives in math, science, and language arts mark significant cooperation in curricular direction. One such initiative, the common curriculum for what is termed English Language Arts,[6] appears to suggest a significant shift in how non-print media and technologies are positioned within the sphere of concern of this curriculum subject. This position, outlined in the validation draft document *Foundation for the Atlantic Canada English Language Arts Curriculum* (1995) is what I address here.

Within the Foundation document, educators are guided toward a notion of "what it means to be literate in the twenty-first century as visual and electronic media become more and more dominant as forms of expression and communication" (1). The document is quite explicit in its well-intentioned move to broaden notions of literacy practices and literacies practiced:

> As recently as one hundred years ago, *literacy* meant the ability to recall and recite from familiar texts and to write signatures. Even twenty years ago, definitions of literacy were linked almost exclusively to print materials. The vast spread of technology and media has broadened our concept of literacy. To participate fully in today's society and function competently in the workplace, students need to "read" visual texts (such as illustrations, photographs, film, and video) and use a range of technological forms of communication. For these reasons, the curriculum at all levels extends beyond the traditional concept of literacy to encompass media and information literacies, offering students *multiple pathways to learning* through engagement with a wide range of verbal, visual and technological media. (1–2)

The predominance of a skills-based approach to literacies—the texts that must be decoded by skillful readers—is clear here. Thus, while the range of texts to be read and the literacies to be developed is expanded, the conceptual terrain of literacy is not. Most obviously missing is the *cultural subject/body* of literacy, that body constituted in and of literacy practices.

The writers of the Foundation document prepare educators for this curricular shift by providing extrapolated (re)definitions of *text* and *representing. Text* is defined as

> any language event, whether oral, written, or visual. . . . The term is an economical way of suggesting the similarity among many of the skills involved in "reading" [various media and] . . . takes into

account how meaning is broadly constructed and mediated through a range of texts. (ii)

The term *representing* "is used to suggest the range of ways in which students create meaning . . . [the f]orms and processes of representation students use to explore and communicate their understandings. . . . (ii) In these ways, the curriculum document maintains a structural model of language (see Chapter 1) as expressive and transparent, and a constructivist theory of meaning as individually made. Of further note is the emphasis on the media and the meaning, not the meaning-maker (or the meaning *made* of the maker). The reader has been disembodied and vacated; identity, as an effect of the negotiation of meaning, appears to be conceptually beside the point.

Under the guise of change, then, already institutionalized so-called progressive literacy practices are reinshrined through the cooptation of some of the *terminology* of a postmodern and poststructural theory of language (see Chapter 1) with no attention to the fundamental and radical shifts such a theory demands based on its social premises, its version of selfhood, or its philosophy of meaning. These inconsistencies are further betrayed by the rationale presented for a focus on multiple literacies, those of fuller societal participation and workplace competency. These "old lies" and clichéd dreams are of those whose interests have always been served by particular and similar notions of literacy. It is here that the focus on skills subordinates the social work of literacy, disguising in whose interests practices of literacy are mobilized. Following the line of argument presented in this document, what will it mean to move beyond print literacy to multiple literacies? That those educated will be better *consumers* of these technologies and the meanings they command? If so, as curricular goals, they smack of hypocrisy and seem inseparable from the marketing mechanisms of corporations for whom the language used to describe the conditions and dreams of the disenfranchised becomes the slogans by which to access greater market wealth.[7]

At this historic juncture—one of widespread redefinition of curriculum directions at the end of the millennium—it would serve the many others whose interests fall to the margins of the present societal order if curriculum goals encompassed clearly how specific *enabling* literacy practices might be pursued within this movement toward multiple literacies. Expansion of the range of media to be "read" is insufficient if this movement is not accompanied, simultaneously, by development of modes of analysis and critique that support literacy practices to enable possibility, to challenge inequity, and to urge redefinition of the world rather than mere participation in it as it is now structured. Such objectives demand the examination of how culture is engaged and how literacies are practiced in specific contexts and for specific purposes.

Yet, within this Foundation document, popular culture is not mentioned at all and culture, where it is mentioned, is written as stable and within the realm of tradition—something had, not negotiated. Popular culture, the single most influential cultural force in the lives of the students to whom this document will ultimately speak, is not mentioned at all. Such absence aids and abets the denial of pleasure, politics, and identity as in/formative and as the necessary focus of a curriculum within the postmodern.

■ Cultural Pedagogies

The influential pedagogues of the twentieth century are not simply the hard-working teachers of the public school system: they are the hegemonic cultural agents who mediate the public cultures of advertising, radio talk shows, the malls and the cinema complexes. It is in these representational domains, fashioned through powerful forms of address, that the intersection of unmet needs and the mundane desires of daily life are made concrete.

—Henry A. Giroux (1994, 45)

[E]ducational theory must engage with the popular as the background that informs students' engagement with any pedagogical encounter.

—Scholle and Denski (1993, 307)

The insights accessible through cultural studies and its methods of analysis should be of particular interest to educators concerned with broadening the domain of literacy practices and literacies practiced. First of all, popular culture, as Scholle and Denski point out above, is the backdrop of the encounters of students with school culture and knowledge. Roman and Christian-Smith (1988) provide a more expansive view of the point, capturing the dialectical relationship of school culture and popular culture beyond a mere backdrop effect: "School knowledge must be understood relationally in its intersection with the knowledge and meanings acquired and constructed outside schools in other institutional and informal contexts" (21). To understand more fully this dialectic—to understand how students engage school knowledge—and to engage the complexity of existing student knowledge, affective investments in the popular must be validated *and* critiqued.

Secondly, because the popular is often the site on which identities counter to those legitimized by schooling practices are constituted, its engagements and meanings are of paramount importance to a more democratic schooling project. This importance goes beyond what meaning is made of schooling within the popular; it extends to what is being said, more generally, about the regulation of experience and the horizon of hope. Popular culture is the site on which the dreams, desires, fears, and anxieties of youth are articulated. Through its "perpetual pedagogy" (McLaren and Hammer 1992, 33), popular culture is also a powerful means through which identity is constituted and desire is structured. How are such processes mobilized and negotiated? What politics inform what maneuvres and meanings of culture? These questions weigh seriously on any meaningful engagement of future possibility for youth.

Yet, a curricular focus on popular culture is not without its problems and contradictions. A major source of concern is in the objectives attached to the study of the popular. Conservative, liberal, and radical approaches to popular culture differ. While each approach might offer a valid argument for the study of popular culture, the political agenda of each would differ significantly. A conservative approach might stake out a reactionary agenda, focusing on the study of the popular as a means of rigidly moralizing its toxicity and bolstering a knowledge to aid and abet further moral and social regulation. Liberal approaches to the popular are also problematic, for they sometimes offer a patronizing openness that denies rather than confronts its own politics. As well, liberal approaches can, in the words of Giroux and Simon (1989), "become a form of voyeurism or satisfy an ego-expansionism constituted on the pleasures of understanding those who appear as Other to us" (25). Radical approaches, while constituted on the basis of the contradictory politics of pleasure, must also address their valorization of the popular and of pleasure as well as the "educational colonization of the popular" (A. Luke 1993, xi), that is, the development of *schooled readings* (see Chapter 1) of the popular.

This latter problem, the inevitable schooling or disciplining of popular culture through the curricular gaze, requires some address. The political importance of the popular lies in its position as an alternative site for the construction of meaning *against* institutional forms. An educational institutionalization of the popular threatens to detonate its resistant character. This factor, alone, is often the major *point de resistance* for students when popular culture comes under educational scrutiny. Indeed, this phenomenon is often used by educators reluctant to engage popular culture in classrooms as a rationale for their nonengagement. Such a tactic, while appearing altruistic, actually refuses a challenging pedagogical dynamic. Failing to engage the popular presents an educational loss to everyone involved, for it bypasses an opportunity to examine how culture, power, desire, and identity intersect in all our lives. From the perspective of literacy education, such nonengagement of the popular detours the thorny issue of readings and political investments, avoiding the problem rather than working with it.

In relation to the popular, as with other cultural sites, an important focus is to analyze and to critique the location of readings, their affective investments, and their political effects. This focus provides for an articulation of comparative readings, sites, and investments: *terms* of *engagement*. Such analysis and critique would, then, provide the basis for an understanding of the terms of resistance of the popular without an attendant agenda of cooptation and diffusion. This approach to the institutionalization of the popular can disavow the abdication of responsibility by educators, while it can also refuse the conservative inclinations of even radical pedagogical agendas for the popular that might suggest "the desire for forms of mastery" (Walkerdine 1990, 174) of particular expressions of agency. Fundamentally important to a realization of the pedagogical usefulness of engaging the popular is the development of the basis on which all involved can address the constitutive and contradictory dynamics of affective investments in the popular from points of difference within social struggle. Only then can affective investments in social change become a pleasurable politics, an aspect of which is insight into the political effects of popular pleasures.

Cultural studies attempts to address such dynamics of popular cultural practices. It approaches all cultural practices—popular reading, television, popular music—to discern how they are more complex, and more deeply problematic, than what tired and often uninformed elitism can capture. Challenging the false divisions between so-called high and low culture creates a space to examine this complexity, to study how it is that texts speak to, of, with, and against one another, so as to expand meaningfully the project of multiple and *enabling* literacies. Its thrust is toward a view not only of how our pleasures fail us, but also of how these pleasures provide for possibility and empowerment. The shift implies that it is no longer defensible to fall back on taken-for-granted notions of "standards," value, and "discriminating taste" to guide us culturally. Educators must look more closely at the *full* implications— at the level of culture, identity, and power—of the narrow selectivity that has accompanied literacy education in media generally, within the print medium specifically, and, overall, through the perspectives taken to each and all.

What might this attention to popular culture mean for the teacher of literacy? Or, put differently, what can the literacy educator *do*? First and foremost, literacy educators must be vigilant readers of culture ourselves. There are at least two prerequisites to this: an acknowledgement that *culture counts*, that it is educational folly to ignore popular culture both because of the problems it poses and the promise it offers; and, ongoing professional development in teaching and reading popular culture. There is now a strong emerging literature that addresses children, youth, and popular culture. Yet, it would seem that much of it has failed to transform literacy education. Ongoing professional development in the teaching and reading of popular culture entails recognizing the established position of such study and availing of the methods of analysis and insight provided therein. Better-educated cultural critics are better literacy educators. It is an indefensible educational position to refuse to teach about popular culture because of attitudes that pose as discriminating taste but that are, in reality, thinly disguised elitism. The task is to educationally *engage* popular culture; there is no requirement to personally *embrace* it. Still for all, popular culture constitutes not only the backdrop of the lives of youth; so pervasive is its presence, it forms the backdrop of all our engagements with the cultural world.

An essential component of rigorous cultural analysis within literacy education can be found in the poststructural practices of *semiotics* and *deconstruction*. *Semiotics* is the study of signs and their meanings. As Carmen Luke and Geoff Bishop (1994) note, "[w]e are all practising semioticians, daily reading and negotiating a world of symbols, and constructing ourselves semiotically: from the way we dress to the way we communicate non-verbally" (111). *Deconstruction* is the process of undermining the systems of opposition and difference that underlie signs and their meanings. Identifying and undermining the relational interdependence of meaning and difference is the project of deconstruction.

As part of a political project of *resignification*, the remaking of meanings of, for example, feminine subjectivities (see Chapter 5), readings of culture based on semiotic and deconstructive methods hold invaluable potential. However, *deconstructive semiotics* (Luke and Bishop 1994) alone, as helpful and important as it is, is insufficient. *De*construction alone can foster despair. *Re*construction, the remaking of culture in ways that educate social consciousness, and which often draw on postmodern methods of parody, irony, and inversion, can foster hope that social change is possible, feasible, and pleasurable. Such focus on cultural production that a resignifying project necessitates allows for a reclamation of the local within a global network of cultural hyperbole. Such alternative productions of culture indicate sophisticated syntheses of critical popular literacy skills, which pose empowering pedagogical positions.

It is an all too obvious point that if curricular objectives are directed toward multiple literacies, then literacy educators need employ multimedia to develop such literacies. Opportunities are needed for students to produce their work in various media, in other words, to write in various media and to read and be read through various media. An "insistence on the letter" (Green 1993)—a rabid print-centrism held in place through the avoidance or refusal of postmodern culture—accomplishes a stalwart but anachronistic notion of literacy. For those who fear that such diversity of media might erode further already diminishing traditional literacies, it is worth considering the benefits a recognition of the increasingly hybrid and inter-discursive character of all cultural texts might accrue in literacy education. Educators might wish to avoid establishing a politically convenient either/or binary between print and other media, which automatically privileges print and subordinates any other media in relation to it. Literacies are interdependent; the meaningful pursuit of multiple literacies locates print *in relation* to other media. This internet user captures the point well:

> High minded critics grumble that "youth are part of a post-literate generation," yet they ignore that thousands of us are scraping together $30 a month for the privilege of being able to read and write through the internet. So maybe we really are a literate bunch, but we're not much impressed with what the traditional print media hype has been supplying the last few years. (Mamer, *trip*, 1995)

The project of multiple literacies is not to move beyond print but to move along with print into broadened notions of what it means to read and what it is that can be read. However, it is not sufficient merely to diversify media. No amount of multimedia in and of itself will sufficiently enhance the critical capacities of media readers and writers. Only rigorous, farsighted literacy education that is multimedia based will accomplish that.

Part of the debate therein would focus on issues of technologies, readings, and culture and what political investments of culture the debates represent. In other words, these questions are ongoing; the answers are always contingent. Herein lies the need for a pedagogical caveat. If literacy educators want to engineer the surrender by students to certain ideological positions presented by educators, failure is inevitable. It is the hardline position often taken by literacy educators toward the culture of youth (when it is taught at all) that creates resistance to such teaching of popular culture. Such rigidity tends to simplify rather than amplify the complexities of culture and power. Effective pedagogy designed to clarify the ties that bind us to culture and to show the ways in which identity is negotiated through cultural engagement needs to proceed in another way; it must attend to the contradictions of culture through honest dialogue that may not necessarily know on what side it will emerge. This notion is, in part, what Lawrence Grossberg (1994) refers to as "a pedagogy of articulation and risk" (18). Grossberg further describes it as

> an affective pedagogy, a pedagogy of possibilities (but every possibility has to risk failure) and of agency. It refuses to assume that either theory or politics, theoretical or political correctness, can be known in advance. It is a pedagogy which aims not to predefine its outcome (even in terms of some imagined value of emancipation or democracy) but to empower students to begin to reconstruct their world in new ways, and to rearticulate their future in unimagined and perhaps even unimaginable ways. It is a pedagogy which demands of students, not that they conform to some image of political liberation nor even that they resist, but simply that they gain some understanding of their own involvement in the world and in the making of their own future. (18)

Such pedagogy may appear more politically unsafe but, in its praxis-oriented openness, it is also more sound.

The popular will continue to provoke us, to entangle our desires, dreams, and fantasies with the promise of pleasure *and* the gesture of resistance. A healthy suspicion of *all media*, including print, is essential in the development of a critically literate populace. A critical popular literacy involves reading vigilantly the sociocultural and economic dimensions of our *engagements with* culture. Addressing adequately the violent representations of women, for example, must include addressing the often contradictory investments of those who engage these representations and how such representations actively structure the desires and fantasies of both men and women. These insights are not available to us if we simply ignore popular culture, or if we look to popular culture only to establish surface traits that then become the basis for ignoring it.

Popular culture is the most powerful pedagogical tool of the postmodern world in that it is both complex and uncanny in its ability to engage, to shape, and to define desire. Literacy educators, the "cultural cartographers" (McLaren and Hammer 1992, 31) of the postmodern, need be as pedagogically savvy and provocative. The "hearts and minds" sought, fought for, and colonized under the tenets of modernism are now the subjects/bodies of culture within the postmodern. A pedagogy of culture, based in interrogative analysis of the interrelationship of subjectivity, culture, desire, and power, that is, a pedagogy that moves beyond mere text analysis into the larger dynamics of cultural engagement—how the body embraces, is in braces by culture— poses greater educational possibilities within the postmodern.

■ From Text to Body

Literacy education informed by cultural studies and that proceeds from a pedagogy of culture is reoriented toward an examination of the production of subjectivity through specific cultural practices. In previous chapters, Peter McLaren's notion of enfleshment (see Chapter 2) and my notion of embodied literacies (see Chapter 3) were highlighted in order to emphasize the acute bodily site of subject formation and/in literacy practices. A reorientation of literacy education toward cultural studies further entails developing an investigative stance around culture, refusing its obviousness, and focusing, instead, on how culture proceeds definitionally at the level of the subject body. A pedagogy of culture is concerned not only with unveiling the intricacies of textual meaning, although this is an important component of cultural analysis, but also with revealing the workings of cultural texts as embodied "modes of intertextuality" (McLaren 1995, 64): the interplay of subject, text, and context.

In keeping with the educational promise of the popular and in anticipating the address of the next chapter (see chapter 5)—the schooling (disciplining, regulating, shaping) of feminine bodies/subjectivities— this section is focused on the place of the body in cultural studies. Specifically, I speculate on directions for cultural studies and education that bear a certain urgency of address given current thrusts in popular culture. Of particular interest, in this regard, is the kind and character of attention to the body of youth in marketing culture. I want to focus here on both the body as a site of antidemocratic sentiment and constitution and the body as a site of resistance and recuperation. Underpinning these foci are questions of the relationship of the body to the project of schooling, the place of *body talk* in schooling practices. In other words, what questions might cultural studies in education ask about the in/scription of bodies? How might cultural studies in education re/mind understandings and practices of the body as cultural site, political force?

Three movements within popular culture, at first glance, appear to draw radical attention to the body in culture: the representation of bodies previously absent, disguised, despised, or diseased such as those of lesbians, gay men, transsexuals, persons disabled, persons of color, and persons with AIDS; the increased practice of body marking and piercing; and, the heightened representation of the fascist body ideal, particularly in art and advertisement. These representational practices, while apparently distinct and even contradictory, raise questions of the political impetus that drives them and the extent to which this political impetus is shared by even apparently contradictory practices. In other words, these practices raise pedagogical concerns about the interrelationship of culture, representation, power, desire, and identity, that is, the *terms of engagement* of such representational practices.

The first of these practices, the increased representation within popular culture of socially marginalized bodies, appears to counter a politics of exclusion. Indeed, the impulses of inclusion should not be approached only cynically. While it is the case that media representation is not often or always accompanied by legal, civil and human rights, an overt cultural presence does diminish the distance of difference. The other side of this proximity, however, is erasure through homogenization. A liberal sprinkle of socially marginalized bodies is not, in and of itself, a radical countering of the hegemony of White, male, heterosexual, abled bodies of culture. To the contrary, a scratching of the surface of the postmodern's apparent penchant for difference often reveals a powerful but less apparent consumption of difference. That is, the inclusion of difference can often be an effective means of subsuming difference. Popular gestures that speak *alike but differently* can have the pedagogical effect of erasure of the struggle of difference, that is, the social conditions under which difference is equated with subordination (see chapter 6). In such cases, those differenced bodies become exoticized markers, keeping company with but never in the same company as those marked by the signifiers of social dominance.

The second, the increased practice of body marking and piercing, raises more provocative questions. The body has historically been used as a cultural statement of status and position, a provocative reminder of how meaning (w)rests on the body. However, the contentious issue of the body as a potentially radical text, as a site on which the dominant disciplining mechanisms that inflict the body are challenged, is more pronounced within the postmodern where bodies are, on the one hand, more evident and, on the other, are often more evidence of how the bodies, while counted in, do not count. Peter McLaren (1995) devastates aspects of both postmodern and poststructural analysis as

> complicitous in the devitalization and derealization of the body, and its reductive cancellation; furthermore, they solemnly strip bodies of intentionality and volition and their capacity to resist the image systems which help shape their subjective awareness. It is a position which maligns the lived body as a material referent for the construction of oppositional subjective forms, material practices, and cultural formations—what I call "zones of emancipation." In effect, postmodern culture has taken the body into custody where it has become liquidated to the currency of signs. It is as if the flesh has been numbed in order to avoid the unspeakable horror of its own existence. (64)

The criticism of non-agency afforded postmodernism and poststructuralism is now well established. However, the scenario of the custodial body, while hyperbolic, is no less disturbing. The practice of body-piercing may be one place where custody is registered as threat, as not-yet-accomplished: a site of hope.

The following example may demonstrate some of these subtle contradictions. A recent advertisement for the Canadian music video channel, *MuchMusic*, features a close-up photo of a partial (from diaphragm to hip), apparently White and gender-deceptive, but likely female, torso. The torso is nude but for a glimpse of the waistband of blue jeans and, less obviously, underwear. The button of the blue jeans is superimposed with the *MuchMusic* logo. The navel, on which the photo centers, is pierced with a pendant of the *MuchMusic* logo. At the top of the torso are the words *Alternative Medium*. I use this advertisement to draw attention to the contradiction it encodes: the body as the ultimate site of resistance; and, within the postmodern, the body as the final frontier of regulation—the virtual-ly borderless body.

The *MuchMusic* advertisement, first and foremost, reiterates the intimate relationship of music, particularly rock, and the sexualized body (Shumway 1989). The advertisement cashes in on the resistance to bodily prohibitions instituted elsewhere, for example, in schools, which constitutes much of youth engagement with rock. Further, it (literally) forefronts the body as the site of identity, where mediated culture comes to (w)rest. However, what the advertisement also accomplishes is the resignifying of the body, itself, as medium, as object, *and* as *point de resistance*. Certainly, McLaren's claim of the body being "liquidated to the currency of signs" is evidenced here, the body pierced with commodity logic and denied its gendered markers. Yet, the advertisement simultaneously and contradictorily promises pleasure as it flaunts unfeeling. The pleasure/pain nexus captured therein pronounces the dissipating frontier of the body and its capacity to participate with feeling in the postmodern world. If the piercing pronounces the body as increasingly renouncing pain while the body also signals the pursuit of pleasure, the body is a nihilistic sign in servitude to the postmodern world. But to what extent is this sign in protestation, pierced against as well as pierced through with commodity logic? The body as sign is staged alternatively, both as an *alternative medium* and on the site of an *alternative medium* (*MuchMusic*). Both media are complex and contradictory and must be read for urges that defy the despairing finality of accomplishment.

My final focus, the increased representation of the fascist body ideal within postmodern culture, is directly linked to the erasure and/or exploitation of difference signaled in the initial two focuses. Richard Golsan (1995) points to the reemergence of fascist aesthetics in contemporary advertisements of, for example, Joop and Georgio Armani products. While clearly reinscribing the masculine body as cultural ideal and, simultaneously, further subordinating the feminine, a fascist aesthetic threatens other forms of difference, as well. To what extent, and in what precise ways, is this body aesthetic located within and accompanied by other fascist sentiments manifesting themselves in Western democracies? For example, how might this reemerging fascist aesthetic of the body relate to expressed and heightened fears of difference? What forms of subjectivity are relied upon and pedagogically produced, and in what ways, as an audience for such an aesthetic? What relationship of ideology and the body is promoted? What counter-discourses and subjectivities exist? How are they mobilized educationally?

These questions and others become the focus of a cultural studies in literacy education, which attends to the body as a cultural site. In a postmodern culture, any threat to difference requires vigilant critique and action; "bodies that matter" (Butler 1993) is, after all, an ongoing political and cultural project.

■

The insights provided through a cultural studies focus in literacy education are varied and exciting. They form not only a reorientation to literacy—what can be read, in what ways, and by whom—but also the basis for further questions designed to continue the refusal of any obviousness and to counter the subsumption of difference. Taking seriously how culture works through its relational and representational character on and through the subject/body demands such interrogation and critique; navigating postmodern culture necessitates it. Literacy educators might wish to avoid implication in the social cost accrued in any shirking of responsibility to engage these concerns through multiple, critical, and popular literacies and literacy practices. The two following chapters, each, in ways, concerned with the production of difference, address more extensively some of these concerns and responsibilities.

Five

THE DREAM'S MALFUNCTION

The Back Alleys of Desire

[S]chools constitute sites of *cultural politics* organized through modes of semiotic production that employ various cultural technologies for representing, displaying, and facilitating the mediation of knowledge claims about the world and ourselves. Thought of in this way, schools are tantamount to "dream machines," sets of social, textual, and visual practices intended to provoke the production of meanings and desires that can affect people's sense of their future identities and possibilities.

—Roger Simon (1992, 40)

■ Following the notion of schools as *dream machines* set forth by Roger Simon, this chapter focuses explicitly on the extent to which dominant schooling practices are implicated in the production of specific forms of what I call disarming femininities. As institutional distributors of knowledges or discourses of meanings, the discursive practices of schools position students and teachers variously. Such discourses and discursive positionings are never singular or noncontradictory but are, rather, always multiple and often conflicting. However, schools—and their partner cultural institutions—are remarkably adept at producing consistent, if not invariable, versions of dreams. I also want to argue that schools are implicated in, if not solely responsible for, the production of subjectivities—the subjects and dreamers of dreams, those who participate in any actualization of school-sanctioned visions of the then, now, and not yet.

Following Michel Foucault, many educational theorists have pointed to the ways in which schooling practices discipline the body (Luke and Gore 1992; Shumway 1989; Grumet 1988; Corrigan 1988; Martusewicz 1992; Walkerdine 1990). As in any discussion of desire, so, too, in a discussion of the body, a qualification of breadth beyond sexualization is necessary. David Shumway's summation of a central point of Foucault is particularly succinct:

> The body for Foucault is not a euphemism for the sexual, and *desexualizing* (emphasis mine) is only one aspect of the way the body is constructed in schooling. The body is used by Foucault to indicate the fact that disciplinary controls are not merely memorized or accepted, but actually form the body itself. One could say that they are habits in the sense that they work without the conscious choice of an individual but are ingrained in the very posture and musculature of the body. (Shumway 1989, 227)

Madeleine Grumet (1988) notes that "the gradual and orderly surrender of one's body is the project of the elementary school" (111). These practices of disciplining the body are always gendered; particular forms and practices of masculinities and femininities are the objective. The production of femininities—feminine subject positions—is my focus in this chapter.

Discursive practices discipline the female body in the sense that the positions they offer are regulatory, that is, they regulate what it means—and how one is—to be feminine. Sexualized femininity, then, a dominant subject position for woman *cum* sexual object in a sexist/heterosexist social order is literally worn on the body, embodied. The disciplining of the body accomplished by schools, for example, can then be interrogated for the ways in which it is a pedagogical practice, a practice that propels a specific political relationship between knowledge, power, and identity. Through institutional practices, i.e., policy, pedagogy, curriculum, what do schools *teach* about sexuality, power, and feminine subjectivities? What are the effects of such teaching, whether intended or unintended? How might such effects challenge and suggest implications for schooling practices?

Such questions offer not only a place from which to critique the taken-for-granted practices of schooling and the moral authority they inscribe. More provocatively, such questions insist on a rearticulation of the notion of the *student body* of schools. Against the dominant version of the collective, homogeneous student subject of the school—a school citizen/individual, as it were, the rule and regulation of whom promote the maintenance of a particular gendered and racialized social order—another version of the student body must unfold. This student body would be positioned and expressed in multiple ways; it would address its own constitution and that of Others; and it would know better the terms of its own inscription.

The ideas presented in this chapter focus on such questions. In some ways, this chapter continues a discussion of some of the issues explored in Chapter 2. As there, here the notion of *enfleshment* is crucial to defining the impact of discourses on the body through the constitution of subjectivity. This chapter differs in its focus in that it attempts to heighten the sense of urgency for a particular educational project given the peril for women in dominant practices. This chapter also addresses the accountability required of schools as sites of the selection and sanction of desire, discourse, and subjectivity. Focusing on how schools implement, through its disciplining practices, a "curriculum of the body" (Lesko 1988, 123) through its social, textual, and material practices disavows any separation of the lives of girls and women and the positions of possibility offered through schooled subjectivities. In particular, a revisit of the schooled-girl body and the relationship of literacy practices, specifically, to this construction forms the basis of a discussion of accountability of (school) dreams and their malfunctions.

▪ Schoolgirl *Exotica*

As a means to galvanize the discussion of feminine subjectivities, desire, and schooling, I produce a reading of *Exotica*, a film by Atom Egoyan (1994). I chose *Exotica* as a means to engage, through my reading, a series of pedagogical questions. *Exotica* is an intelligent, provocative film, one rich with signification (as well as significance).[1] Every prop, word, and movement in this film is heavy with meaning. Further, the film's antagonist, in all her guises, demands my attention as a feminist educator. In this regard, I focus on the critically overlooked, downplayed, and underexplored choice Egoyan makes as a filmmaker/storyteller: to place clearly and unequivocally at the heart of his exploration —as fetish and focus—a *school*girl. If, in culture, no representation is incidental, then the choice of subject and the nature of representation of the subject are important questions for educators to address.

My reading of the film is offered here as one engagement, one possible reading negotiated on the basis of discourses available to me and those encoded in Egoyan's presentation. In a sense, then, my reading constitutes what Lynne Joyrich (1995) calls "an ethnography of an audience of one" (59). Here, I am mindful of my own discursive limits, my own locatedness, yet I present my reading not as a definitive critical statement but as a place from which to ask particular questions. Sandra Taylor (1993) notes that "'[r]eading' a media text can be seen as a dialogue between the text and a socially situated reader" (130). The situatedness on which I focus is my work as a feminist literacy educator interested in questions of schooling, culture, representation, subjectivity, and desire. In particular, I want to focus these questions around a dialogue with the film that addresses ways of looking (gaze), issues of knowing, and the politics of difference, recurring points in my (and others) reading of the film.

The internationally acclaimed *Exotica* is Atom Egoyan's sixth film and the first to move beyond more esoteric arthouse audiences to capture widespread appeal with general audiences in Canada and the United States. To explain the appeal of the film, critics have pointed to its well-structured, tightly interconnected, and viewer-friendly narrative line, to the strong casting of familiar, fallible characters, and to the stylistic control and effectiveness of Egoyan's writing and direction. It is not possible to determine fully and adequately the matrix of pleasure and appeal, particularly from the singular reading offered here. However, it is worth exploring that some of the appeal of the film may lie in how Egoyan's very frontal address of an underbelly of desire intersects with, disturbs, and, perhaps, even ignites viewers' desires. In other words, the film *works*, at least for this viewer, because it provokes a problematic gaze while, and as a means of, simultaneously critiquing that gaze.

Unlike many readings presented within cultural studies, my reading of *Exotica* is not constructed primarily from a position of explicitly pleasurable engagement; rather, and more personally problematic, it is prompted by a *fascinated disturbance*, which my engagement with the film effected. This contradictory blend of fascination—the eye of the voyeur—and disturbance—the eye of the critic—is important for it re/minds or re/inscribes the voyeuristic gaze as always both without and within, a deeply internalized practice of looking, not easily disrupted by the critical intellectualization of the problematics of pleasure. Fascination and desire, as Angela McRobbie (1994) points out, are complicitous feelings, which can overspill into hostility toward and/or love of difference. My point is that fascination is a learned gaze, one that is both cinematically used and disrupted in the film. The powerful seductiveness of the film is, in part, due to how the film's gaze rivets through deliberate, understated, and lingering shots, speech, and movements.

Yet, in the end, the gaze holds, its devastating effects seeping subtly but surely into this viewer's psyche. The film trades on the very fascination it stirs to engage a striking commentary of the relationship of gaze and (unwanted) touch.

"*What is it that gives a schoolgirl her special innocence?*" With this line, Eric (Elias Koteas), an emcee/dj at the lavish exotic dance club from which the film in part, derives its name, begins his introduction of Christina, a dancer whose persona is that of an adolescent schoolgirl. As the music of Leonard Cohen's unrelentingly dark "Everybody Knows" builds in the background and as Eric continues to question and simultaneously to weave the fabric of schoolgirl innocence, Christina (Mia Kirshner), clad in white shirt, tartan skirt with matching tie, black stockings, and flat black shoes, and carrying a black satchel, emerges from backstage. In some senses, the heart of the film is encoded in this scene. The song alerts the issue of knowing—who knows what about whom and about what—and its related ambiguities, deceits, and disguises.

Christina's attire signals the specificity of subjectivity and, as her dance unfolds, the choreography suggests the trauma of sexual violence. The repetition of this scene works to return the viewer consistently to the implications—for the schoolgirl body/subjectivity—of all else in the film. In his initial introduction, Eric refers to Christina as "firm, young flesh inviting you to explore deepest and most private secrets"—"the sassy bit of jailbait." This introduction, combined with the fatalism of Cohen's first line, "[e]verybody knows that the dice are loaded," create a psychic *mise-en-scène*, which swells and darkens as the film unfolds into a complex study of the tensions and ambiguities between voyeurism and violence, secrecy and knowing, fantasy and reality, obsession and longing, and alienation and belonging.

The schoolgirl introduced to us by Eric is a fictional figure in a sexual fantasy, one of many women in the dance club, Exotica, who are paid to engage the fantasies of its White, middle-aged bourgeois male clientele. Christina's dance is always the same: She enters the stage, discards her satchel, and begins a provocative dance, which begins with gestures of girlish pouting and boldness, then moves into a subdued mime of what might be a bedroom abuse scene in which a child is awakened and violated, and ends with frantic, distraught arm movements. Christina's schoolgirl persona becomes more startling and increasingly complex in the face of her relationship to a regular client, tax auditor Francis Brown (Bruce Greenwood), to the club owner, Zoe (Arsinee Khanijian), to Eric, and to two other very real schoolgirls: the first, Lisa, the murdered eight-year-old daughter of Francis; and the second, the younger Christina, herself. The mysteries of these relationships unfold in a tantalizing, anticipatory play of signification in which the viewer is implicated as, one after another, expectations, appearances, preconceptions, and assumptions disintegrate and resignify, coaxing from the screen narrative a maddening, disturbing, and intricate web of intrigue and desire.

Despite the linearity of the plot of *Exotica*, due to its several interconnected layers it does not encapsule easily. Francis, the grief-stricken tax auditor, visits the strip club regularly to watch Christina and, then, to employ her at his table as his private dancer. It is in the intense scenes of private dancing that viewers come to realize the therapeutic purpose of this fantasy—although, until very close to the end, we assume the therapeutic relationship is one-way, for Francis only. While he is at Club Exotica, at home, Francis employs a house-sitter, Tracy, the daughter of his brother, to "baby-sit" his memories: his murdered daughter's baby grand piano; several pictures of his African wife and the daughter, Lisa, in the schoolgirl attire in which she was found murdered (and exact to that of exotic dancer, Christina). During one of his visits, Francis is urged unknowingly to participate in a setup by Eric, Christina's jealous ex-lover, who encourages Francis to break a club prohibition and to touch Christina while she dances at his table.

As a result of his impropriety, and in keeping with Eric's intent, Francis is barred from access to Christina and his fantasy. Unable to accept the banishment, Francis bribes a gay male pet store owner, Thomas (Don McKellar), whom he is investigating for illegal importation and sales of exotic animals, into helping him. With Thomas's help, Francis learns of Eric's setup and threatens to kill him for having taken Christina away from him. As Christina dances for Thomas, outside the club Francis encounters Eric, who identifies himself as the member of the search party who found the body of Lisa. In a richly symbolic simultaneity, Eric and Francis embrace outside the club as a home movie shot is intercut of Lisa, her hand held up to block the gaze of the camera. Inside, meanwhile, Christina repels Thomas's unwanted touch, of her own accord, as Zoe looks on from the emcee platform. The full significance of the latter scene is unclear until the very end when in a flashback scene, the younger schoolgirl, Christina, Lisa's babysitter, implies her abusive home life to Francis as he drives her home. The film ends as the younger Christina, satchel in hand, walks into her suburban, middle-class home, closing the door behind her as the camera gazes on.

As the social base of desire, everything has an exchange value in *Exotica*. The flash of bills, or their equivalent, is one of the most often repeated motions in the film. And, just as it is the men who are the desiring subjects in the film (with the exception of Zoe, who, despite her successful contracted insemination by Eric, clearly desires Christina), so, too, it is the men—bourgeois White men, in particular (again with the exception of Zoe)—who are most often the purchasers, in one way or another, of the objects of their needs and pleasures—the Others. In this way, then, the film appears to draw on traditional discourses around the intersections of class, gender, and desire. At the club, it is only Eric who is distinguished by class; it is his body (his semen) that is commodified and his desires that have little outlet but frustration and physical violence. At the same time, though, the final shot of Christina's home, the middle-class icon of civility at the heart of modernism, challenges powerfully our traditional senses of (bourgeois) moral order.

More subtly, the film utilizes equally traditional and disturbing discourses to construct race and difference. Thomas's penchant for exotica goes beyond his pet store stock to a series of men of color, to whom he sells pre-performance ballet tickets and, thus, acquires seated company at performances. This construction of color as exotic Other has a more insidiously violent side not only in the murder of eight-year-old Lisa but also in the suggested dynamics around her parentage. In both the pictures and home video footage that are interspersed throughout the film, Francis's wife is shown to be clearly of African descent. The probability of her affair with Francis's brother, the now wheelchair-bound (symbolically emasculated?) Harold (Victor Garber), is fed not only by rumor and the circumstances of her death, a car accident in which Harold was her passenger and in which Harold was disabled, but also by the suggestion of the allure of Blackness for Harold—an apartment above a Jamaican patty shop, t-shirts promoting Black power and culture. That Harold may have been Lisa's biological father haunts Francis as it haunts the film. But what are viewers to make of the death of both Lisa and her mother? About the easy disposal of Thomas's ballet partners of color? About the eradication of all characters of color? About the relationship of race and desire?

More pointedly, what are viewers to make of a film that constructs such a direct and disturbing relationship between male voyeurism and the murder and abuse of schoolgirls? What pedagogical work might such a film do? To what pedagogical necessities might such a film point?[2] Neither Eric's repeated question in his introduction of Christina—"what is it that gives a schoolgirl her special innocence?"—nor Francis's grief-stricken plea to Christina—"why would someone want to do something like that?"—can be sufficiently answered without solidly linking real violations—real, lived social practices of abuse and murder—and constructed (and lived) social fantasies of desire. Egoyan's film addresses how these fantasies are constructed and within what cultural ideologies and assumptions. In this sense, it is important to address not only what the schoolgirl signifies in the film but what the schoolgirl signifies more generally, preceding the film, as it were, that may have prompted its choice as a signifier at all.

Michelle Fine (1992) argues that the public and educational discourses of female sexuality focus, for the most part, on violence and victimization: "[E]ducated primarily as the potential victim of male sexuality, [the adolescent woman] represents no subject in her own right. Young women continue to be taught to fear and defend against desire" (32). The construction of the innocent schoolgirl serves not only to repress female desire but, also, and paradoxically, to entice predatory practices of male desire. That *Exotica* taps these conventional discourses is unquestionable; yet, the film also powerfully rebuffs dark secrecy, voyeuristic gaze, and unwanted touch. In the second-to-last scene, when Christina removes Thomas's hand after he inappropriately touches her as she dances at his table (another action also set up by the jealous Eric), a viewer is able to read this act as signifying greater control and power for Christina, an act put into fuller signification by the suggestion to Francis of her sexual abuse in the final scene: Christina is learning to refuse her abusers. However, such significance is also slighted against the greater backdrop of fantasy, desire, and power created by Egoyan, and is galvanized in two riveting scenes: the flashback scene in which Eric, as a member of the search party and in the company of Christina, discovers Lisa's school-uniform-clad body; and the final scene of Christina's middle-class home resignified from (the appearance of) propriety to (the lived reality of) perversity. The two brief glimmers of female desire between Zoe and Christina cannot counter the overwhelming trajectory of eroticized violence and difference out of which the film itself creates longing. Indeed, in each of these instances, it is Zoe's desire that is evident; it is as if Christina, throughout the film, has been fetishized into an innocence outside of her own desire—the petrified object of male desire.

Even within the context of suggested woman-desiring-woman, the overtones are less liberating. Is the very pregnant Zoe the symbolic mother (in the face of the absence of all other mothers in the film) who now protects Christina—unlike the mother who may have been unable to prevent or to confront Christina's abuse? And what of the sexual desire between the two? Is Egoyan suggesting a female libidinal rein-vestment in the mother (through other women) as an alternative to the violence of heterosexuality or as a consequence of such violence? If so, how are such signifieds reconciled with the overt reiteration of the hegemony of masculinity in the scene outside the club in which Eric and Francis embrace, the gun Francis had planned to use to kill Eric now resignified as phallic brotherhood as it lies against the middle of Eric's back, at the center of the embrace? And what of the gay Thomas, who is (symbolically) released of both his father's gun (emasculated), when Francis takes it to kill Eric, and of the exotic eggs (potency) he has smuggled into the country with the help of a customs officer *cum* lover? The film does not resolve any of these questions, but it does raise them through how Egoyan chooses to align the film's signifiers. In this way, while falling short of a radical reassessment of sexual desire, Egoyan positions the viewer to ask old questions anew. And by placing a school-girl at the center of the reassessment, he urges a multi-institutional accounting of the constitutive and constituting faces of desire that does not exclude that place of the construction and regulation of "school-girlness"—the schools—toward which the school uniform, worn by both Christina and the murdered Lisa, persistently gestures.

What, then, are the implications of the questions raised by my view-ing of *Exotica* for those who actively participate in and who are con-cerned about how the culture of schooling impacts on subjectivity? On what grounds might the discourses and representations out of which *Exotica* is constructed—discourses that directly address and embody aspects of social class, gender, sexuality, and race—be interrogated and redefined? How might the issues of gaze, knowing, and difference raised by the film inform educational debates? What forms of literacy might position young women and men to read and to challenge such significations and to resignify desire more firmly on their own terms and in their better interests? What practices may effect the breaking of the culturally embedded alliance between violence and sexuality?

■ Literacy, Subjectivity, and the Lives of Girls and Women[3]

If literacy is about "empowerment" through acquisition and critical awareness of "the word," and if women are subjugated through our sex-ualization—that is, the manipulation of our desire to be "feminine sub-jects" who are, by definition, not independent, intelligent and educated—

and if the boundaries of education are set so that literacy and sexuality shall never meet, then what does literacy as empowerment for women mean?

—Kathleen Rockhill (1993, 337)

Literacy and sexuality have always been deeply connected, less explicitly, in the way that Rockhill (1993) contends in the opening quote of this section and, more explicitly, in cultural media. Advertisements for literacy often appeal to the anxieties and desires inscribed in the dominant moral order in an effort to appeal to the advancement of literacy. For example, an advertisement circulated widely in Canadian current affairs magazines (with a largely middle-class male readership) in the early nineties by *ABC Canada*, a national literacy organization, darkly aligns the two. In large letters atop a close-up photo of a preschoolgirl child who clutches a stuffed bear as she is encircled by the arms of a male parent who reads her a bedtime story, the advertisement admonishes, "Make bedtime *story* time." The anxiety signified here, intended or not, finds its place in a discourse of literacy that fantasizes an equation between education/literacy and sexual safety. Within this discourse, high incidents of sexual abuse, assault, and incest are often *negatively* correlated—on the basis of myth and ideology—with low levels of education, a correlation that pathologizes the poor and the working class. Literacy herein is seen, functionally, as a means of social mobility and, culturally, as a means of (sexual) discipline. Oftentimes, the political base of such anxiety is a patriarchal order in which young girls and women are seen as sexual prey and men are seen as sexual predators.

The prevalence of such discourses that trade on sexual anxieties and fears raises important questions of how such anxieties are culturally distributed and what educational challenges their dominance presents. A dimension of the mythology that Atom Egoyan critiques in *Exotica* is the very one supported by the pathologizations effected by such discourses. Yet, their dominance has institutional bases in media, education, religion, and culture. For my purposes in this chapter, and in keeping with the focus developed in my reading of *Exotica*, I attend to the bases these discourses have in schooling.

In an important essay addressing sexuality, schooling, and adolescent women, Michelle Fine (1992) identifies three dominant discourses of female sexuality that circulate in public schools in the United States. Therein, she names three discourses of female sexuality: sexuality as violence; sexuality as victimization; and sexuality as individual morality.

The implied feminine subject of each of these discourses is a passive, dependent object of (male) desire, not a subject of her own desires. Fine contends that missing within the discursive frameworks of public schools is "a discourse of sexual desire and social entitlement" (48). This absence, I contend, betrays any pronounced concern for females as an oftentimes unintentional means of maintaining what I earlier referred to as disarming versions of femininity.[4]

According to Fine, a discourse of sexual desire and entitlement would promote "legitimate position[s] of sexual subjectivity" (41) for adolescent women, provide a critique of the discourses of violence, victimization, and individual morality and the subject positions they offer adolescent women, and promote enabling practices, that are, for adolescent women, "sexually autonomous, responsible and pleasurable" (41). As bell hooks (1992) points out, "asserting sexual agency" (74) is even more problematic for women of African heritage whose sexual subjectivities bear the imprint of White racism. Yet, hooks and Fine share a similar feminist agenda of advancing versions of feminine subjectivity that, as hooks (1992) states of radical Black female subjectivity, "place erotic recognition, desire, pleasure, and fulfilment at the center of our efforts" (76).

The points made by Michelle Fine are directed toward, although not only applicable to, public schools and are limited to the public school curriculum of sexuality education. I want to argue, in concert with other feminist theorists (Rockhill 1993; Whatley 1988) that the points made by Fine have implications for all curricula, including that of literacy education, my focus here. The discursive positions to which Fine refers are produced and reiterated in schooling practices, generally through institutional policy, pedagogy, etc. For example, Valerie Walkerdine (1990) has shown how child-centered pedagogy produces a specific de-sexualized subject position that pathologizes what it suppresses—sexuality—as a condition of producing such a subject. If the *normative* subject position offered girls is one in which passivity, dependence, and sexual abstinence are encoded, then difference becomes aberrant and pathological. Schools, by denial, suppression and pathologization, situate (to use Fine's phrase) a discourse of desire—and the subject positions it offers girls—as inappropriate feminine positions.

While such discourse analysis and subject positions relate most clearly to the objectives of literacy education in curriculum, it is not often the case that literacy educators acknowledge the relationship of the goals of literacy and feminism or of schooling as text. This lack of acknowledgment of any relationship must be seen as a *denial* rather than an absence of such a relationship between literacy and sexuality education. If literacy education is about the production of literate subjects, these subjects are *gendered* subjects. Feminine subjects are also sexualized subjects. Regardless of the extent to which schools might attempt to counter such positioning, the rabid sexualization of female subjectivity through popular culture would still require address (see Chapter 4). It is often the case that schools, rather than countering disarming femininities, proceed as if these subject positions are *givens* requiring compensatory measure (*women are victims; we must learn to protect ourselves*), thereby denying their construction within discourses of the sort outlined by Fine (1992); or schools deny the existence of these positions or that they are the concern of schools. Such denials not only further the production of disarming feminine subjectivities but also prevent educators from confronting the implication of schooling practices in the production of such disarming positions. A critical literacy that embraces feminist goals and that refuses the literacy/sexuality divide would name such denials and direct itself toward pedagogically counter politics of subjectivity.

The discourses of violence and victimization that Fine (1992) outlines most strongly inform the film *Exotica*. As I suggested in my reading of the film in the previous section, Egoyan does appear to raise the issue of women's desire, albeit briefly, a slighting in keeping with the "missing discourse" of desire to which Fine (1992, 31) refers in her essay. Yet, Egoyan's critique appears to be more with the positioning of male subjectivity within these discourses. For, ultimately, it seems, Egoyan *implicates* a particular male gaze—and the social, cultural, and economic practices that support and sanction it—and places this gaze powerfully and unequivocally as the focus of his critique. This critical position is clearest in the alignment of Christina's refusal of Thomas's touch and the flashback to the actual moment of home-video making when Lisa blocks the gaze of her father's video camera. Its darkest and most constant reminder are the female-torso-shaped two-way mirrors that line the Club Exotica.

By addressing the gaze that drives the touch, Egoyan is also pointing to the structuring of fantasy as a key component in understanding relations of (sexual) power. Whose fantasies are represented is one issue; another is how Others are positioned within such fantasies. The exoticization of difference (see Chapter 6) and the relations of power at the heart of this practice are strikingly obvious in *Exotica*. What is also clear is that the production of largely White-male fantasy, through popular culture, media, etc., is implicated in the lived realities of objectification and violence in the lives of women and other Others. It is not that the film suggests a causal relationship between fantasy and expressed violence; it is, rather, that the structures of fantasy and desire—evoked through ways of looking and representing—and the subject positions and lived experiences of women and Others exist *relationally*.

If the relational base of fantasy and desire is so exploitative, the relationship of gaze and touch must be one of responsibility. As Egoyan constructs it, it literally speaks a statement of resistance: *stop the unwanted gaze; stop the unwanted touch*. The viewer is told in Christina's account of Lisa's murder that Francis was implicated, only to be later found innocent. Yet, Egoyan forces the question of who, exactly, is *not* implicated in the gaze of (sexual) objectification and its consequences. If we are all implicated in the construction of a particular and dominant gaze, it is also the case that, within the film, only the women are shown to counter it. A single subject opposing the apparatuses that support dominant ways of looking, i.e., media, popular culture, etc., hardly allows for much transformative potential. Furthermore, a position of agenic response by women defined primarily to prevent and/or to stop violence rather than to pursue more empowering—and desiring—subject positions for ourselves is fundamentally problematic.

Another form of implication also haunts my reading of *Exotica*. If, as many theorists have argued, part of the project of schooling is the disciplining of the body, and if such disciplining (necessarily) enacts a series of suppressions to accomplish desexualization, what might be some of the consequences of these suppressions? Part of what *Exotica* suggests through its fetishization of the schoolgirl is the eroticization of absence, the sexualization of innocence/desexualization as the paradoxical effect of the practice to contain that very effect, itself. Here, the satchel, uniform, braids, etc., become fetishized items that signal what is only apparently missing: the schoolgirl as sexual being. As Valerie Walkerdine (1990) points out, the "impossible fictions" of innocence and "well-behaved passivity" (121) are designed to maintain a "moral order which is threatened by the sexuality of children and the desires of adults" (120). Egoyan's film shows us the darkest consequences of such denials and suppressions.

But of what concern are such issues to literacy educators? In the context of the overwhelming and constant colonization of culture in the postmodern and the uncanny ability of "cultural cartographers" (McLaren and Hammer 1992, 31) to encode exploitation beyond the obvious, only a particularly vigilant literacy education will do. If the postmodern puts representation and difference foremost on the cultural agenda, literacy educators must put multiple forms and practices of reading, representation, and culture foremost on its agenda. Ultimately, if reconstructing the world is to be a possibility, we must first and foremost be able to read the insidiousness with which the world is socially and culturally constituted. Such reading requires attention to more than print culture and to more than a skills-based decoding practice. As McLaren and Hammer (1992) argue,

> [n]eeded is a counterhegemonic media literacy in which *subjectivities may be lived and analyzed* (emphasis mine) outside the dominant regime of print culture—a culture that is informed by a technophobic retreat from emerging technoaesthetic cultures of photography, film and electronically mediated messages. (62)

Literacy educators ignore poststructural attention to discourse and subjectivity and postmodern attention to culture and representation to the real peril of those constituted exploitively therein. The "everyday pedagogic events" of image, sound, and print consumption more profoundly affect the meanings of lives than most of what it is that schools currently address. Without address, the dominant discourses of femininity and sexuality will continue their work of mining disarming subjectivities. With address, the positions of subjectivity and the desires and dreams to which they gesture, may be (re)read and rewritten in difference.

Critical citizens of schools, the student body urged forward in the introduction to this chapter, can only be produced through an awareness of the social and cultural world as textual, as reading to bodies, as requiring read of and, finally, as readings *on* the body. The social and cultural world is always embodied, its meanings are carried on the body, which is, itself, a social and cultural site of struggle within and against this social order. Questions of the nature of gaze and sexual objectification, victimization and violence point to the need for literacy practices or ways of reading the cultural representations through which ways of looking are constructed and deployed. This focus is an integral part of any project of critical literacy that addresses what Bronwyn Davies (1993) calls "the systems of thought through which [students] are shaping their desires" (146).

■

The questions raised through my reading of *Exotica* around the issue of difference, the position of the Other within culture and schooling, require much more sustained commentary and critique. The postmodern focus on difference does not secure a transformative politics of difference; to the contrary, the impulses and effects are oftentimes toward homogenization. The focus of the next chapter is an articulation of a project of and about difference and desire formulated through a politics that simultaneously counters dominance and celebrates the possibilities of difference.

Six

WITHOUT MIRRORS

The Project of Difference

In the sense that it is premised on a perverse advertisement for a common culture populated by an enforced tolerance for difference, schooling too often becomes an alibi for not exploring otherness, for not engaging in a politics of difference. It becomes an alibi for not desiring.

—Peter McLaren (1995, 233)

■ To address a politics of difference is a first imperative of a transformative educational project. The issues of difference, as they were briefly raised in previous chapters, point to the centrality of language, literacy, representation, and culture in the reiteration and/or countering of destructive or diminished difference. The intersection of desire and power, within the wide-spread frameworks of capitalist economy, compulsory heterosexuality, White supremacy, and male privilege, often produces desire that advantages or maintains these frameworks. The promise of pleasure at the root of such hegemony is the persuasive means by which the Other is sustained by the cultural gaze from without and within. In other words, desire and difference intersect in identity. These concerns, formulated toward a pedagogy of difference with a particular emphasis on racialization, are the focus of this chapter.

The initial efforts of colonized peoples[1] to claim a space in the architecture of culture—representation in various media—can often be described as efforts to create flattering mirrors—positive reflections of the experiences of the colonized, produced by the colonized them-selves—with which to counter the negativity of the absent or refracted images represented by the colonizers in their own interests. Similarly, other marginalized groups—women, lesbians, gay males—strove for representation to which they were signatory as an initial stage of claim-ing public space. These efforts, often directed at naming the "authen-tic" experiences of the "essential" subject—usually formulated through the singular standpoint of gender, race, social class, or sexuality— appealed to the heart of liberal humanism as they constituted a demand for a place of dignity and shared justice within a "common humanity." At this *fin de siècle*, we continue to throw off the dark legacies of what was another century's enlightenment; the project of social difference, which may be described as that of confronting, redefining, and charting anew what John Willinsky (1994, 616) calls "the moral economy of rep-resentation," with its implications for cultural identity, poses itself as more complex, less straightforward than these earlier ones, and fraught now with the anxieties of a postmodern age.

Cast in theoretical *post-isms*,[2] the "crisis of representation" now addresses "difference" and "the Other" as the crucial points of constitu-tive subjectivities whose range of possibilities is delimited by social positioning and ideological sedimentation. In a rapid fire of theoretical advancement, the promise of liberal humanism has been revealed as illu-sory in the face of the realizations of the political underpinnings of social difference. Thus, the contested discourses of, for example, multicultur-alism, cultural diversity, cultural plurality, and antiracism, the theoreti-cal roots of which are in liberal humanism, have been supplanted by a discourse of difference that challenges the fundamental informing assumptions of these other discourses. As Chantra Mohanty (1994) points out, a discourse of difference must reconceptualize the issues,

> so that differences can be historically specified and understood as part of larger political processes and systems. The central issue, then, is not one of merely *acknowledging* difference; rather, the more difficult question concerns the kind of difference that is acknowledged and engaged. Difference seen as benign variation (diversity), for instance, rather than conflict, struggle, or the threat of disruption, bypasses power, as well as history to suggest a harmonious, empty pluralism. On the other hand, difference defined as asymmetrical and incommensurate cultural spheres situated within hierarchies of dominance and resistance cannot

be accommodated within a discourse of "harmony in diversity."
(146)

In this measure, difference must be understood as culturally constituted within relations of power, that is, regulated through discourse and meaning, which are, themselves, imbricated with these very relations.

Yet, to avoid the assimilationist argument that difference must be dissipated to accomplish social justice, it is important to note that difference is not only a political and social necessity; it is also a signifying necessity. Difference is a condition of social and political processes. But difference is a condition, at once, of language and of desire. A significant point then becomes how to recognize how difference works—what differences, with what effects, and on whose terms. These issues of signification, of personal and collective significance, are defined and fought over on the terrain of culture and/in representation. The self—and collective determination of "what differences" becomes the sought-after goal in a context of cultural multiplicity where difference is not managed, transcended, or abhorred but, rather, exists within a practice of cultural challenge, contingency, and change—where and as necessary in an unrelenting struggle for social justice.

■ Signifying Difference: Identity

Language is the site on which identity is sculpted, the subject's claim to sign-ificance, its place of difference within a system of signifiers. In this sense, identity may be understood as a condition of both containment and claim, a contradictory space of regulation and possibility. Given the relationship of language and desire articulated previously (see Chapter 2), identity may be understood as a cultural manifestation of the desire of the subject for a coherent self and the reiteration of significance claimed and forged within language. Coward and Ellis (1977) provide a useful elaboration of this (Lacanian) notion of identity with/in language.

> The signifier, then, is seen as the mark of separation by which identities and difference can be established. It is not, however, a simple matter of the subject learning to ascertain relations of contiguity and difference: it is also a matter of the subject's own identity being achieved by this same process of differentiation, marking out of separations between itself and its own surroundings in order that it may find itself a place in the signifying chain. (98)

Thus, identity functions to order the subject so that participation in the social and symbolic order, positionality in language and discourse, is possible. It is difference that makes identity possible.

Because the symbolic order, of which language is a part, is already structured on the oscillating tensions of privilege and privation, some differences are historically implanted as more alienating than others within the signifying chain. Teresa Ebert, in formulating a postmodern feminism (1991), clarifies this point:

> To say that language is the arena of social struggle and that difference is a political difference is to say that difference—difference within, [Derrida's notion of] differ*a*nce—is always "difference in relation"; in other words, difference within is always "difference within a system." (897)

Identities, then, are not forged through personal and psychic claims only; and such claims are never formulated outside the political dynamics of the social and the symbolic that mediate all signifying claims. Thus, control over the signifiers of one's identity is not autonomous. Arranged in social relations of difference, signification is such that meaning can be imposed on a signifier and historically sustained through the institutionalization of discourses, which secure the structures of dominance and that govern meaning.

In this respect, identity is socially imposed as it is also personally or collectively composed. For example, the meaning of woman, Black, or lesbian is not determined solely or even largely by the subject(s) occupying the said identity position(s). Rather, meaning is a product of the discourses of identity available and accessible in a given historical moment. It is in this way that social identities can be constructed to sustain dominance. An often-cited example is the historical construction of Whiteness as a political category to unify certain European colonialists and to rationalize their difference from and imperialist domination of African and aboriginal others (Jay 1995; West 1993; Mohanty 1994). Discursive power is used to maintain these categories and the dispositions of privilege and privation that accompany them. That is, the (false) binary out of which a signifier comes—woman/man, Black/White, or homosexual/heterosexual—and on which each term in the binary depends for meaning, is not socially balanced. Within the binary, a dominant term (man, White, heterosexual) signifies not only social power for those who approximate the identity category but also greater significatory power, that is, power over how one's signification/significance is represented and understood. Identity, then, is an ongoing achievement of difference within an already structured symbolic order and, as such, the subject cannot but incur the costs of placement within that order—displacement, self-alienation, incommensurability, the very conditions of entry into language.

Yet, it remains the fundamental contradiction of identity that it is the pursuit of difference and significance driven by the desire for sameness, to see oneself reflected back as whole, coherent, and in community with same (yet different) others. In its common usage, the word *identity* (from the Latin *idem*, meaning same and the French *ite*, meaning the condition or quality of) relies on this contradiction as it is also suppressed in the name of identity politics. While personal identity marks a difference from others—individualization—collective identity marks out collective sameness, at the expense of unshared or suppressed difference. For example, earlier stages of feminism relied on a collective, undifferentiated notion of "women" and "women's experience" that ignored differences consequent of class, race, sexuality, etc. The solidarity such single-minded differentiation was meant to build found itself worn thin by differences, which challenged the definition and conditions of collectivity feminism was attempting to build.

A more glaring example of how difference is used deliberately to sustain particular subject positions, in this case, of nationalism, can be found in the 1995 Quebec Referendum Campaign in Canada[3]. As part of the Yes Campaign for a Sovereign Quebec, the provincial-ruling separatist Parti Quebecois attempted to utilize such difference to its own ends. The *coeur quebecois* advertisements were a series of posters that targeted the "visible minority" population of Quebec. Two posters, in particular, reveal the convergence of difference with an essential nationalism: One poster featured an Asian-Canadian woman and a caption, "Almond Eyes, Quebec Heart"; another featured an African-Canadian man and a caption, "Dark Skin, Quebec Heart." In both posters, particular racialized differences are highlighted in an effort to display the diversity that is Quebec nationalism and to counter claims of racism as a persistent feature of this nationalism. The linguistic essence that remains undisturbed by the poster representations reveal the assimilationist sentiments of the nationalist movement as it also reveals the very hybrid character such nationalism cannot afford to admit and can only accommodate as threat. The appropriation of difference in this case is a management strategy with overtones reminiscent of Huck Finn and another century. This old politics of difference is founded in a colonialism that relies on binaries and essences to rationalize its own continued practices of hierarchization and exclusion. At the "heart" of such nationalism is difference mediated in the interest of the dominant.

The call for a "new cultural politics of difference" (West 1993, 203) in recognition of "the new politics of identity" (McRobbie 1994, 53), in which multiple difference is specifically signified under a common signifier, is in part a decry to tease out the contradictions of identity as part of a political project of social justice, at the heart of which is the symbolic order articulated through issues of representation, culture, and identity. In the project of the new cultural politics of identity, the range of constitutive identities is displayed, reconstituted, and contradicted across an open, ongoing social multiplicity that resists the very tendency toward homogenization, which the "as a" claim evokes, even as it is evoked to mark (still further) difference. The excessiveness of identity claims is the product of formulations of identity wherein the spillage, the excess, that which does not fit the norm as evoked, becomes the insistence of a renewed identity claim. In this sense, then, within the new politics of identity, there is an inherent paradox: refraction as inevitability, as necessity built on the indeterminability and instability of the signifier.

■ Desiring Difference

At one point in her discussion of "teaching to support unassimilated difference," Elizabeth Ellsworth (1992, 4) asks, "[w]here do our desires and expectations that 'difference' be rendered 'meaningful' come from, and whose interests do they serve" (7)? This question, the question of desire and (the conquering of) difference, is at the heart of the educational project of difference. The process of education—enacted on many pedagogical fronts from public schools to popular culture—based as it is in imperialist, colonialist, and, now more than ever, consumer ideologies, produces subjects whose positions within these indentured relationships ensure the appropriation of difference through a tourist model[4] of knowledge and longing, which ultimately ensures the maintenance of such relations (Willinsky 1994; McLaren 1994a; hooks 1992). The voyeur-tourist, whose consumer longings and paternalistic inclinations ensure that "difference sells" to those who can afford to buy, is the new po-mo consumer who struts the Other without acknowledging the exploitative relations on which these consumptive habits are built. Here, desire is assimilative, consensual, constructed on the terms of the dominant at the expense of the Other. Postcolonial enterprises strive to confront this consumer, and undo the relations of power that secure servitude. Here, postcolonialism faces off against "consumer postmodernism" (Giroux 1994, 4) and the struggle over representation and identity.

In a 1995 interview, Richard Rodriquez[5] commented rhetorically on the apparent contradiction inherent in the United States government's practice of cuts to immigration quotas (a common trend in the West) at a time when the national character of the United States is increasingly recognized as that of the immigrant:

> How do I account for the fact that, at a time when black and white relationships are so difficult in America, blond kids are listening to rap? Within what is desired is also what is feared. The stranger is the figure of the American but also the threat to American stability. (Bernstein 1995, 77)

Rodriguez, here, reiterates a point made by many scholars, that fear is "a central constituent of a politics of difference" (Walkerdine 1990, 208) and, further, that desire can contain psychic expressions of fear of difference.

The hybridization of cultural identity to which Rodriguez alludes is increasingly obvious within the postmodern, where "the allure of ethnic difference" (Bernstein 1995, 88) has created a culture in which many people, especially youth, "choose" identity and mark it through fashion, speech, attitude, music, and lifestyle. Indeed, such hybridization may be one of the most obvious and wide-spread popular manifestations of the crisis of identity and the desire for difference. For this reason, and because of the youth population in which it is most readily manifested, I want to examine the phenomenon of hybridization to address further the connections of desire, representation, identity, and pedagogy.

I do not begin from the assumption that what Angela McRobbie (1994, 192) calls "fragile, 'shaggy,' hybridic identities" are characteristic only of the new and fashionable faces of colonization and appropriation. With McRobbie, I see such invention as agenic, hopeful, and potentially transgressive. Nor do I question the substantiveness of hybrid identities, in particular those based in historical experiences previously effaced, forgotten, or denied and those created out of global movement, diasporic conditions, and shared struggle. While realizing the uncontainability of any categories, I here differentiate between these (re-)*emerging* hybrid identities and *consumer* hybrid identities, those negotiated largely through consumer desire rather than a politics of struggle, reclamation, justice, and a politics of reidealization. While these two categories are not mutually exclusive, as I will point out, political possibility and effect distinguish their currency in a project of difference. Prior to any avid celebration or rejection of this particular form of hybridization, it is necessary to question the precise political terms on which these identities are forged. In any discussion of identity and representation, the question for a pedagogy of difference is less one of legitimacy than it is one of the extent to which chosen hybridization might transgress and/or suffocate difference. In a wholly postmodern manner, hybridization mocks any notion of authenticity or essence, to pose, instead, a contingent subject-in-the-present whose surface is also its substance. In an ironic reversal (sans the painful politics) of members of racialized groups "acting White," these (often White) youth are "disclaiming White" in response to postcolonial discourses that have challenged its hold on (the subjects of) history. Yet, the effectiveness of such critique—where parody is the effect, if not always or often the intent—is highly questionable.

If, as Richard Rodriguez (in Bernstein 1995) suggests, a desire to not only consume but to become the Other is a habit of fear disguised as longing, such hybridization can speak more to greater colonizing tendencies than to any real counter tendencies, i.e., decolonization. In such cases, the response by colonized groups can be to reassert political needs from more fixed, linear, and modernist positions. Particular cultural practices that emerge from African-American communities are common examples for hybrid market activity. bell hooks (1992) comments on a response to such commodification:

> [B]lack nationalism surfaces most strongly when white cultural appropriation of black culture threatens to decontextualize and thereby erase knowledge of the specific historical and social context of black experience from which cultural productions and distinct black styles emerge. (30)

Such retrenched positions demonstrate the potentially retrogressive effects of the appropriation of difference. While the line is often blurred between appropriation and appreciation of difference, exchange is a condition of learning and coalition-building. This exchange cannot be demanded, though, given how racism shapes cultural vulnerability and makes protectionism desirable (Johnson 1995). Desire that is based in practices of transgression (hooks 1992) designed to alter relations of power clearly holds greater possibilities than those designed to maintain colonialist ideologies. Identities designed in the marketplace rarely fulfill, even while the desires that make them popular commodities at all clearly hold, such promise. As Henry Giroux (1994) notes, the challenge is "to address the politics of identity in pedagogical terms that rewrite the discourses of commercialism *and* separatism (emphasis mine)" (60). Such critique provides the opportunity for chosen hybridity to move beyond appropriation to become enlivened with a radical political energy that has the potential to truly make a difference.

The issue for educators, then, is to transform the legacy of schooling to meet a postcolonialist agenda. With respect to a politics of difference, this transformation entails confronting how the meanings of difference are represented in the popular as "texts of desire" (see Chapters 4 and 5). Prior to that, however, it entails schools coming to terms with precisely how it is that desires, identities, and difference are managed through the practices of schooling and how such practices deny transformative education for what Peter McLaren (1995) calls "a perverse form of prohibition in which desire as human agency is not permitted to explore its own constitutive possibilities" (233). This reflection is the work of all educators, yet it seems especially pertinent to, although certainly not the exclusive domain of, literacy.

■ What Difference

The parasitic relationship of the categories of difference (West 1993)—that difference is a relationship and a relationship of dominance and dependence, at that—is the key to grasping what exactly specific differences signify and what counter-discursive strategies might work most successfully as part of a resignifying project. Forged under the conditions of the signifier—instability, ambiguity, contradiction—identity cannot be fixed, unequivocal, or fully present in the subject. Identity is always contested, partial, and contingent and its foray is the field of culture, the everyday, lived and represented. Cast in this way, the project of difference is clearly *pedagogical*; that is, the making and remaking of identities is an ongoing production founded on the intersection of specific discourses of culture, history, knowledge, and meaning.

Much recent educational literature attempts to address "the difference difference makes" in the struggle for democratic schooling and, in particular, the attainment of forms of literacy. Many scholars write from a particular identity politics to address "what difference makes what difference." As a result, there are now available accounts of the relationship to literacy of such social markers as gender/sex (A. Luke 1993; Horseman 1990; Rich 1986), race/culture (Ferdman 1990; Delpit 1988; Gates Jr. 1985; Ogbu 1983), and sexuality (Rockhill 1993). These accounts exist alongside a literature that addresses more generally the crucial issue of "literacy and the politics of difference" (Giroux 1993,

367). One thread that connects all these accounts is the assertion of the connection between literacy and identity: that, in fact, "making identities" is, in large part, what the project of literacy is about. In this section, I will explore further the project of difference as it relates to critical literacy and the question of identity.

If identity is carved on the frontiers of culture and representation, knowledge of the workings of these relations—among identity, culture, desire, and representation—is essential to any form of self-determination in the face of contemporary hyper-colonizing processes. Yet, a concerted effort to achieve a literacy in which questions of representation and knowing are politicized has not been seriously undertaken in public schools. Often preoccupied with skills acquisition and, in secondary schools, located within a vicious circuit of canonic texts and practical criticism, educators often see difference as a sensitive issue best left unnamed or as a sensitivity issue resolved through celebratory discourses that neutralize the power base of difference and exoticize its manifest content—positions encouraged by dominant discourses of multiculturalism, cultural diversity, and cultural pluralism. The retrograde effects of such positions are painstakingly evident in the escalating tensions between communities of differences and the schools to which the responsibility for their educational well-being is legislated. In the face of this divide, the schools have failed to demonstrate an effective response-ability. My contention, here and elsewhere in this book, is that policy and structure changes notwithstanding, literacy education itself must be reconceptualized to address difference in the terms demanded of the crises at hand.

Vigilant counter-readings of culture are also required. By counter-reading, I mean those deconstructive readings that refuse the terms of difference on which a text is constituted. An example may clarify this point: The *United Colors of Benetton*, in their 1996 campaign, used an advertisement that pictured three human hearts, each labeled to represent racial colors—white, black, yellow, and in that order. In typically Benetton fashion,[6] this ad uses a startling image and few words to encode a social statement as a means of highlighting the company and its products, an advertising strategy that has proven to be immensely successful. This ad is not unlike several other Benetton ads, which attempt to promote a superficial notion of equity while simultaneously erasing significant social differences. The "race hearts" advertisement requires little by way of print literacy. By opting for images to suggest "we're all the same on the inside" (more overtones of Huck Finn), however, Benetton is forced to name—and therefore reiterate—the categorical constructs that are the *modus operandi* of racism.

To promote a notion of literacy that enables a reading along with the interests of Benetton, a common approach guided by liberal humanism orthodoxy, refuses to acknowledge the dominant politics of difference that form the assumptions on which the advertisement builds. A more enabling literacy would locate the ad precisely within such dominant discourses of racism and then proceed to challenge these premises by providing counter-readings. Such counter-readings would problematize the categories—and the notion—of race themselves and attend to the daily realities of privilege and powerlessness that accompany the structuring of society on the basis of externally evident traits, realities not relieved by clichés of the sort provided in the dominant reading. Further countering would note the other differences that attention to "color" only supplants, i.e. social class, gender, etc., differences omitted in Benetton's pretence of social awareness. Indeed, the radical question the Benetton ad begs is "If we are all the same on the inside, *why* do some differences make such a difference?"

If a move toward multiple literacies (see Chapter 4) is to be socially enabling, it is essential to recognize that not only are not all readings alike but not all readings are of equal social value. Progressive literacy (see Chapter 1), many times the bane of enabling social criticism, has left a liberal humanist legacy best confronted and discarded. The effectiveness of the Benetton advertisement (for Benetton) counts on the reader having available the dominant discourses of racism and the clichéd responses to it (in Canada, state-sponsored "multiculturalism," for example). These Benetton advertisements make sense only because racism exists; and, the sense they most easily make comes from already available and common discourses from which readings of the problem of racism are constructed. As is, such a literacy is socially disabling and pedagogically uninspiring. It draws from and reproduces the status quo of social meaning and social order. The skills to deconstruct the premises on which such a literacy proceeds and to recognize whose interests are met by it requires a more rigorous and vigilant approach. This approach rests on educators having available to us the critical means to encourage such rigor and vigilance.

The terms of a critical literacy outlined earlier (see Chapter 1) offer a beginning place for reconceptualizing a literacy of difference. However, it is necessary to attend, in particular, to *what* difference what *difference* makes for critical literacies, too. In the past, it has not been uncommon for a notion of critical literacy to encompass a focus on social class to the exclusion or marginalization of gender or, within feminist literacy, to encompass a focus on gender to the exclusion of class or ethnicity. A literacy attentive to competing and overlapping differences, the incommensurability of difference, and difference as social and historical process has a more complex task than that accomplishable through singular standpoints and fixed positions (Brady and Hernandez 1993), one that demands a reconceptualization of literacy and of difference. Still for all, the specific constituents of each position of difference within the overall social construction of differences requires focused attention, too. Thus, it should be noted that to critique the singularity of a position is not to dismiss that position as requiring attention; rather, it is to point to its partiality, the exclusions that can create the very same conditions it is designed to challenge. A literacy of and for difference should surpass singularity for an open-ended multiplicity where meanings are made to quiver with uncertainty.

For those interested in critical literacy, then, the challenge of difference is mammoth. Central to confronting this challenge, however, is the countering of the dominant effect of mainstream literacy practices: becoming Other to oneself. This self-denial, an effect of the absence of positive difference or of the presence of difference as negative, can be a profoundly alienating effect of literacy education. If literacy is much more than functioning within a particular technology, usually of print, and encompasses, as well, the production of subjectivity as the manifestation of oneself in relation to the world, then critical literacy must begin there, with the embodiment of literacy practices and with how it is that all forms of literacy function, without reprieve, in "the authorization of selective versions of textuality, subjectivity and the polity" (Luke 1991, 140). Only when educators encourage the means to such insights as a step to achieving a wider expanse of identities as expressions of human possibility and meaningful difference will critical literacy have begun to meet its social goals.

■ Incommensurable Differences: The Pedagogical Challenge

The necessity of alterity—the interrelationship of self and Other—that much postcolonial and psychoanalytic theory places at the foreground of knowledge production (Simon 1995; Felman 1987) forces a radical reconceptualization of the terms of engagement of difference and their pedagogical implications. Increasingly, progressive educational literature devoted to education and difference points to the need to challenge and transform dominant inflections of identity and meaning that constitute difference as inferior, hateful, exotic, and, therefore, dismissable. A suggested corollary to such pedagogical agendas may be that sameness (as self-love) need not be examined. To the contrary, as the insights of psychoanalysis continue to remind (Silverman 1996), understanding the psychic conditions and effects of identification as sameness and Otherness are instrumental to mounting positive social change. To effect a radical questioning of the historical and political constitution of difference, then, requires a simultaneous challenge to the dynamics out of which all difference, all identity, subordinate and dominant, is constituted, a psychic as well as a social and cultural phenomenon and, ultimately, a pedagogical task.

Because pedagogies designed to address difference are situated and contingent, any attempt to prescribe or formula-ize approaches runs the risk of participating in the very homogenizing tendencies such a pedagogy attempts to counter. To diminish this risk, rather than speak to the specifics of lived pedagogies—ethnopedagogies, if you will, of which there are now many excellent examples, particularly within feminist pedagogy (Lewis 1993; Ellsworth 1992)—I will speak instead to some of the principles that can guide our gestures toward what might be called a curriculum and pedagogy for and of difference.

1. Schools and classrooms are never outside the (re)constitution of difference. To the contrary, these sites have historically been the places from which difference has been solidified in the interest of the dominant. As Edward Said (1989) warns,

> there is no vantage *outside* the actuality of relationships between cultures, between unequal imperial and nonimperial powers, between different Others, a vantage that might allow one the epistemological privilege of somehow judging, evaluating, and interpreting free of the unencumbering interests, emotions, and engagements of the ongoing relationships themselves. (216–7)

Cultural workers located in schools and classrooms need to confront the legacy of difference as we challenge the grounds on which it is constituted, by what means and in whose interests. Such work can only begin with the acknowledgement and understanding of how it is—in what specific ways and through what specific practices—that the work of schooling, curriculum, and pedagogy is implicated in the making of social differences that make an unjust difference.

2. Just as there is no position of epistemological privilege outside

relations of difference, there is also no model available to educators that affords a comprehensive view of the workings of power. Judith Butler's warning of the risk of "epistemological imperialism" (1993, 18) is well worth noting here. While pedagogies to counter the abuse of difference must vigilantly interrogate the workings of all forms of difference and how forms of difference work interrelatedly, such work is always limited by the histories and subject formations of those who do it. These subject histories and formations are never fixed or complete, but they are also only ever partial—and never impartial. The pedagogical conditions of this partiality, its sources and effects, are a constant focus of critical self-reflexivity and redefinition. What our identities as pedagogues both allow and disavow requires constant scrutiny.[7] In other words, the embrace of difference is always contingent, provisional, limited by the very position and reach from which embrace is staged.

3. While the subjection of the Other is the political concern of the pedagogical project of difference, how that subjection is achieved through the experiences of the subject of dominance requires deconstruction. How a subject experiences social privilege is an essential exercise in denaturalizing the constituents of dominance and articulating the circumstances of power that determine the differences on which dominance depends to maintain its normative stance. For example, in addressing racialization, Peter McLaren (1994) notes that it is necessary to interrogate "the culture of whiteness itself" as "an emergent ethnicity." Failing to do so, he argues, reiterates an order that "naturalize[s] whiteness as a cultural marker against which Otherness is defined" (214). Geoffrey Jay (1995) talks about such work with students as part of "a more public reckoning with the relationship between their personal and their group identities" (124). But this is not only the work of students; pedagogical accountability in postcolonial times demands this reckoning of us all, a confronting of what Chantra Mohanty (1994) calls "co-implication," that is, a recognition of and a responsibility for the indictment of *all* social subjects in the processes of racialization, gendering, sexing, etc.

4. Co-implication demands an interrogation not only of the knowledge claims of the identity of the subject in dominance but also of the Other subject. Reluctance by White cultural workers to interrogate the knowledge claims of the Other refuses the complexity of experiences of difference, a practice that can inadvertently reinscribe dominant positions. As Gayatri Spivak (1990) points out, the "Native Informant" does not have access to objective truth, and the "problems of selfhood" (66) are shared by all social subjects. This point should not be misconstrued

to dismiss or to level perspectives. As Spivak (1994) notes elsewhere,

> there are those who have been obliged to cathect the state of the other. Historically, they have always occupied the position of subject in the lower case, they have been subjected so that the other subject can be sovereign. . . . [T]he whole hierarchical taxonomy of concrete experience which has been regarded as completely valid for so long is exactly what has to be got under. At the same time one cannot use that as a terrorism on the people who were obliged to cathect the place of the other, those whose experiences were not quite "experience." (129)

Our shifting positions within discourses do provide access to different mediations of experience. The importance lies in discerning the ways in which any and all accounts of experience are mediated and regulated by the discourses through which they are expressed and the possible positions within them. The availability of discourses and postions as they relate to issues of power then becomes a measure of possibility in a world ordered in and through language practices.

5. Central to a pedagogy of and for difference is the questioning of the grounds on which identity is constituted within specific historical, cultural, and political contexts and redefined as these contexts (demand) change. To question identity is not to erase or to negate identity, although the latter, as a condition of the refusal of identity, can be a consequence of what might be deemed at the time as political necessity. In fact, such refusals are imperative to the disavowal of forms of subjectivity that oppress others and invade their efforts to forge lives of dignity and meaning. Thus, identificatory positions have a powerful ethical dimension, which extends to points of avowal as well as disavowal. For example, charges of the "essentialism" of some identity politics should be weighed in terms of the historical backdrop of genocide, systemic erasure, and denial against which these identity positions are often claimed as well as the positions of dominance and low risk from which these charges are often levied (Spivak 1994; Luke and Gore 1992). That is, claims of essential difference can be contingent political strategies that suspend, not erase, differences within groups. Contending with the hybridity of postmodern identity may be the most effective long-term political strategy; however, historical context may deem it neither readily available nor feasible.

6. The pedagogical project of difference is a resignifying project; the project's genesis is culture, representation, the day-to-day mediations of the everyday returned to us through structures of signification. As a

resignifying project, its focus must be the incommensurability of the signifier and the signified, or what Homi Bhabha (1990) calls "the uncertainty of cultural meaning that may become the space for an agonistic minority position" (317). As educators, our efforts may be best directed at accentuating the gap between the signifier and the signified, to fan the dissent against dominant discursive positions, and to procure a contrary citizenry who refuses to take meaning for granted and whose struggle with the signifier is part of a renewed effort at significance in a less misery-producing social order. Such "cultures of dissent" (Mohanty 1994, 162) herald the hope of postcolonialism, an animated, vigilant project of the decolonization of the Other.

7. As a resignifying project, the project of social difference falls within the realm of literacy, literacy practices, and literacy education. The gross neglect within literacy education of the notions and consequences of difference while its focus of study and achievement is language, representation, and meaning, the very vehicles through which difference is constructed and regulated, is unconscionable. From early school to adult education, a reformulation is required of what it means to "do literacy" in ways that capture its differentiated, contextualized, and politicized practices, its very *everydayness* in culture. Further, inasmuch as systems of signifiers are the domain of all knowledge and its representations, only vigorous cross- and interdisciplinary approaches to critical literacy will accomplish the goal of a citizenry educated to pursue democracy and not only to exist and to be complicit in its present illusions.

8. Reconceptualizing literacy through broader lenses of textuality practices and locating pedagogy itself as problematic textual practice reveals a notion of curriculum firmly rooted in the cross- and interdisciplinarity for which I have argued. Patti Lather (1991) identifies such a notion of curriculum with her sense of a "deconstructive pedagogy":

> Instead of commenting on a text or practice in ways that define it, a deconstructive approach links our "reading" to ourselves as socially situated spectators. It draws attention to the variety of readings, the partiality of any one view, and our implications in historical social relations. . . . Hence, *our reading of the text becomes the curriculum* (emphasis mine), a curriculum designed not so much to oppose a counter-hegemonic meaning system against a dominant one as to ask us to insert ourselves into the discourses that envelop us. Here, we deconstructively explore the relation between ourselves and how we negotiate the search for meaning in a world of contradictory information. (145–6)

The moral foundation of such a curriculum is not abandoned to an eternal play of signifiers but is located in the meanings and actions of everyday life. It is a curriculum the basis of which is "the foundation of *difference*" (C. Luke 1993, 93). Luke defines this foundation of difference as

> [a] construct of difference that extends beyond the monolithic sociological triumvirate of class, race, gender and makes conceptual space for cultural difference in subject location and knowledges [that] renders such a foundation anti-essentialist and indeterminate. The indeterminacy lies in the rejection of unified self-contained knowledges and single-strategy pedagogies. Knowledges and knowing are always provisional, open-minded and relational. . . . (193)

As Luke also suggests, knowledges are also specific and multiple, a concept that moves against the grain of the monolithism that is the basis of dominant curriculum sustained for homogenization and assimilation and against difference.

■ Mirroring the Desires of Difference

[T]he ideal that is mirrored depends on that very mirroring to be sustained as an ideal.
                                                              —Judith Butler (1993, 14)

We need to learn how to idealize oppositionally and provisionally.
                                                              —Kaja Silverman (1996, 37)

The postcolonial subject is not the subject whose emancipatory movement can be described as moving from a subjected position where one is "without mirrors"—lack of representation of the image—to a place in the hall of mirrors—a public, self-determined place on the signifying stage. Rather, it is more an address of the politics of misrecognition created through the illusion of full presence in the context of absence. In part, this is what Kaja Silverman (1996) points to in her argument for learning to "consolidate oneself as a subject of lack" (37). In no way does such a condition of lack diminish the ongoing political necessity of new and renewed representations that encourage the (further) expression of multifaceted identities. In this sense, then, there is the need to utilize the place of misrecognition as one from which to begin to speak of the necessity of difference as a bulwark against erasure while never relenting on the necessity to overcome the destructive disordered difference that the hierarchization of difference makes. Finally, there is the need to refuse the seduction of mirrors and the illusion of coherency, of seeing possibility in refraction as a condition of consciousness, and of learning to live in and with selves divided in and through incommensurable difference.

It might be argued, then, that a poststructural account of difference must always address but never resolve the tension between the desires out of which representations are sought and identities are forged and the inevitable misrecognitions and ill-fits that characterize representation/signification itself. What poststructural theories offer the project of difference is attention to the (im)positionality of the subject in discourse as incomplete, refracted. However, in mirroring fragmentation, poststructural theories can elicit a certain hopelessness and loss of community and identity—shattered mirrors. The recognition of the political necessity and worth of identity and community need not be threatened by fragmentation, provisionality, and contingency. To reiterate an earlier point, to question the constitutive grounds of identity does not entail a necessary negation or abandonment of identity. If the conditions of identity formations are social and political, as well as linguistic, then struggles for a new politics of difference must be staged from these positions, as definitional *and* provisional, as a means to remember, to name, and to struggle to exceed them. Confronting the conditions of our illusions need not eradicate the hope that is the dream of difference.

■

Pedagogy, difference, and transformation as projects of a critical literacy informed by cultural studies, one in which the intersections of culture, power, desire, and identity are addressed, must confront, ultimately, its own modes of persuasion. Increasingly, within radical pedagogies committed to addressing a politics of difference, the eros of pedagogy is a focused problematic. The final chapter concludes the discussion of the schooling of desire by attending to eros, in particular, an eros of radical pedagogy from the perspective of the making of the teacher-subject.

Seven

PASSION DESIGNS[1]

Eros, Pedagogy, and the (Re)Negotiation of Desire

■ An underlying theme of the essays in this book is the importance for educators to acknowledge and to reflect on our cultural engagements or readings of culture as auto/biographical moments, as telltale signifiers of investment, desire, and identity. Engagements with/in pedagogy are an indispensable aspect of analysis of the politics and culture of pedagogy where pedagogy is located within cultural practices of power and design. This note is struck resoundingly well by Alice Kaplan in her memoir, *French Lessons* (see Chapter 3), and is reiterated by several theorists who see the work of schooling and desire as irrevocably bound (Britzman 1992; Taubman 1992; Simon 1995; Grumet 1995; Gallop 1995; hooks 1994; Pagano 1991). The purpose of this chapter is to focus eros and pedagogy, both its more hopeful and darker sides, as that most intimate exchange of pedagogical desire. Unlike the previous chapters—the issues of which were addressed specifically, although not exclusively, to literacy educators—this chapter addresses the cultural work of education more generally.

■

A pedagogy that explores the subjective embodiment of desire and the mobilization of desire in and through social forms and practices will inevitably confront its own claims on eros. While the presence of an erotic character of teaching has been identified in the popular domain through film (*To Sir with Love*; *Lianna*; *Educating Rita*), situational dramas (*Room 222*), and music (Sting's *Don't Stand So Close To Me*; Meg Christian's *Ode to a Gym Teacher*), within educational theory, the notion of eros has been less widely addressed.[2] To trace the sociocultural histories of the representations of eros through such popular formations is not my intention, although I do see such work as a worthwhile and exciting project within cultural studies.[3] Suffice to say here that the popular has been at the forefront in acknowledging and locating a problematic, even if not always problematically.

Part of an explanation for the dearth of educational literature addressing eros and teaching may be found in the general resistance by educators to any acknowledgment of desire and teaching. As teaching subjects, teachers have been positioned within the same discourses of desexualization (Shumway 1989) to which students are subjected. As purveyors of such discourses, teachers are expected to deny eros— which is predominantly associated with the sexual—as part of the particular (bourgeois) ideology of moral order to which schools predominantly subscribe (Walkerdine 1990). Passion and teaching can be connected only if (properly) regulated and channeled—onto content as infectious or into caring as parenting.

The psychic base of learning articulated through psychoanalytic theories of learning and pedagogy (Felman 1987; Gallop 1988; Grumet 1988) poses a less easily regulated and more insidious eros than that which underpins the disciplining project of schools. However, the insidiousness of eros is not a result of eros itself; it is, rather, a result of an educational refusal to look at the relations of desire and power that constitute teaching. This *refusal* manifests itself in an unchecked, unreflexive eros, one that denies the power-full and pleasurable relations of teaching and learning and also reproduces a narrow and uninformed notion of eros itself. This chapter seeks not to reduce teaching to eros but, rather, to recover eros as a multifaceted and complex practice of desire and as a irreducible dimension of all teaching.

■ Engaging Eros and Teaching

The reading of *Exotica* presented earlier (see Chapter 5) was designed, in part, to demonstrate how it is that engagements of cultural texts might form the basis for the useful address of pedagogical questions. In that chapter, my intent was to focus the production, through culture and schooling, of a particular form of subjectivity, that of the schoolgirl. Here, in this chapter, my attention is somewhat different, although the focus on subjectivity is still maintained. My concern is the production of teacher subjectivity and the modes of desire that secure that identity position. My intent is not to address any indefensible monolithism around teacher subjectivity. I am more concerned to pose questions about in what ways culture is implicated in the production of particular notions of (pleasurable) teaching. In other words, what might be the relationship of (popular) culture, desire, and teacher subjectivity. Again, I offer "an ethnography of one," my reading of *To Sir with Love*, as a place from which to address this question.

To Sir with Love features Sidney Poitier as Mark Thackeray, an unemployed engineer who accepts a teaching assignment in London's East End while he continues to search for work in his chosen career. Originally from British Guinea, and having lived and worked in California, Thackeray epitomizes the colonized subject; he is the signifier of what English (British) schooling can produce of those who desire and come to identify with dominant ideology. He is composed, self-disciplined, and "stately"; and he suffers the indignities of racism with quiet dignity for, as he himself is heard to say, "forgiveness is the gift of God." *To Sir with Love* traces Thackeray's efforts to school his brash, angry, undisciplined and mostly White working-class students. His success is rewarded with their affection; and in the end, despite an offer of an engineering job, Thackeray decides to remain at the school.[4] The film has remained popular, particularly among school teachers whose formative career choices coincided with its release in 1969.

My earliest personal sense of eros and teaching represented within the popular domain comes from this film and the title song by Lulu. This often-heard recording kept memories of the film fairly vivid despite the quarter-century elapse since my first viewing. So powerful was the effect of the film, as a preteen viewer, that I remember a range of details of context and feeling that surrounded that first television viewing: the very chair in which I was seated in our family living room as I watched the movie in the company of my father; the necessity of getting permission to stay up to watch it because it was televised late and on a school night; the discomfort, accentuated by the presence of an adult, that I felt at my own feelings of pleasure during scenes in which the affection between Thackeray, the teacher, and the students is clear (feelings my body recovers even in adult viewings, for example, the self-conscious reflex of the downward gaze in such instances—this particular response a text still "written on the body"); and the anger I felt at the students who seemed initially unappreciative of Thackeray's efforts to change them.

Despite my being a schoolgirl when I first watched *To Sir with Love*, I do not recall an strong sense of identification with any of the students;[5] instead, I identified, then unproblematically, with Thackeray, in particular with his desire to help the students, his gracious suffering of racial humiliations, and his struggles to live bourgeois values despite his poor background. Then, I did not consider the mismatch and contradictions of my identifications, a White adolescent woman so strongly aligned emotionally with a Black adult man. I now record their similar occurrence as part of the pleasure of viewing the television show, *Room 222*, with whose main character, the Black high school teacher, Pete Dixon, I also strongly identified. Such female "cross-gender peregrinations" (Silverman 1996, 35) are now a well-documented aspect of feminist film theory. While such female identifications, as Silverman (1996) also points out, "often work only to confirm libidinally the values traditionally attributed to the male body" (35), I do see the cross—race identifications noted here as ones of albeit contradictory possibility.

In retrospect, my own viewing of the film realized two facets of my then only liberal inclinations toward social equity: Just as Thackeray had been transformed so, too, could (and would) I; and, just as Thackeray would do the work of transforming (the gender politics of which are so clearly noted in Lulu's metaphor—"how can you thank someone who has taken you from crayons to perfume?") so, too, could I. With and despite all the attendant contradictions of my own positioning and identifications, the film mapped onto and kindled my own schoolgirl fantasies of adulthood, the transformations necessary to get there, and the kind of teacher I desired to become. In this sense, the film is inserted into my educational biography as both forming and informing.

Of particular interest to me in my recollections of the impact of my first viewing of *To Sir with Love* and its remembered pleasures is how it might help me locate, in part, some of my earliest sources of eros in/and teaching. What forms or social relations of eros accompany desires forged and reiterated through such phallocentric fantasies as this film, but one example in a wide and continuing (although not undifferentiated) repertoire? The production of particular forms of subjectivity, masculinities, and femininities, which are the explicit pedagogical work of Thackeray, revolve around mind-body splits, rationality and sexuality, and discipline and desire. In the film, Thackeray clearly exchanges signifiers of passion, sexuality, and home community for rationality, regulation, and bourgeoisment. These tensions form a metaphoric dance of lack and exchange that, in the end, reiterate a dominant pedagogy and its attendant gendered subject positionings. For me, a girl-child who inhabited what my teachers called the "brawn and brain" dilemma, my identification with Thackeray was particularly pedagogical. This split, as I pointed out earlier (see Chapter 3), especially devastating for women and Others, can become a virtual disappearing act, when the relationship of knowledge and corporeality—the racialized, sexualized, classed, and gendered body—is denied.

The explicit gendering of the fantasy that the film presents is evidenced most clearly in the ways in which submission (female) and resistance (male) are borne out and rewarded. The male character, Denham, who, throughout the film, most strongly resists Thackeray's lessons is "won over" in a boxing match—ritualized bonding—and bestowed the Phallus, the assignment to teach (like Thackeray): the disciplining of the body and the privileging of (masculinized) rationality. The female character, Pamela, who most strongly admires Thackeray and who most clearly attempts to embody the codes of class and femininity he prescribes, is rewarded with the fulfillment of her requests, that he address her by first name and that he dance with her at the closing party. Each request rotates around intimacy and sexuality and is lived out in their dance—the white-clad virgin and the Black man—in which she is delivered to a patriarchal notion of womanhood, the object of desire, and he is delivered to his roots, the (Black) dance of (working) class. Less than ironically, it might seem, this particular bestowment is through a cultural practice—dance—noteworthy for "challenging the fundamental restrictions which schooling puts on the body" (Shumway 1989, 226) and used as such in the film in which the students dance during their school lunch break as part of the opposition to the schooling of their bodies. In my own desirous viewing, I wanted both symbolic bestowals: the (female) intimacy and the (male) social power, desires I now realize were formed in a complex and contradictory dynamic— serial splits—the result of negotiating and maneuvring competing demands from a variety of sources, i.e, family, school, and peers.

This analysis of my engagement of *To Sir with Love* propels at least two questions: What lingerings of such configurations of eros might continue to inhabit my present practices? How might such insights be useful to further the project of radical pedagogies? There is little question that my young and deep desire to be transformed through meaningful teaching and, as an adult, to transform through meaningful teaching, holds me still. Thackeray's credo, *It is your duty to change the world*, resonated loudly if mistakenly in my schoolgirl ears. In keeping with these desires, I became an English teacher, for, of all the teaching subjects, English appeared to offer the ripest ground for such work, that of "cultural missionaries" (Matheison 1975, 210), one of which I was determined to become. However, I do not too hastily claim no vestiges of this former self. In my present work within feminist and critical pedagogies, disquieting moments recur. For example, "conversion narratives" (Munt 1993, 82),[6] in which I am a character, attend my teaching, although they are now somewhat different, inverted almost, and more consciously grounded in struggles for greater mutuality (Simon 1992, 72) than that of the model on which my earlier desires of teaching were, in part, constructed.

Any effects of conversion, any projects of transformation, however well intentioned, committed, and, even, unintentional, should always be viewed problematically. That is, such projects need to be interrogated for the ways in which knowledge, power, pedagogy, and desire intersect in those of us who desire conversion and those of us who desire to be—or who become—a figure in that process. Desires for conversion are produced as particular hegemonic positions within pedagogies. For this reason, and because of the heavy investments teachers and students have in pedagogies, a greater problematizing of what is increasingly referred to as the erotic character of radical pedagogies seems necessary. I see eros as an activating, arousing energy, not necessarily or only sexual, which quickens our sense of our own desires and reminds us of the constituency of our personal and collective pleasures. Where goes desire goes eros. But what discursive traces does eros bear? And what are the implications of those traces for pedagogy?

■ Re/Tracing Eros

Within Greek mythology,[7] the birth of Eros is identified in two separate contexts: within the creation myths, as the first god, the force behind creation; and, later, of lesser importance, as the god of love, the son of Aphrodite, the goddess of beauty and love. In the earliest thorough record of creation (that of the poet, Hesiod), Eros is born of Chaos, a void or gap, and is the impetus for all (pro)creation, the reason Eros is sometimes considered the first god, without whom there would have been no others. His role was to cause completion and unification, through desire: a precursor to future equations of lack and desire. In later myths, Eros is the frequent companion of Aphrodite, her son by disputed paternity. Eros is most frequently pictured as a handsome, winged creature with a bow and quiver. For my purposes here, noteworthy, also, is the marriage of Eros (Cupid) to Psyche, the soul, in which was born their daughter, Pleasure: early forays into psychoanalysis.

The earliest philosophical discussions of Eros complement this history, and my arguments. The Greek Aristophanes is best known for the earliest contemplations of sexual Eros, in which he used a creation myth to pursue the argument that Eros is the energy seeking to recreate our wholeness, which was lost in the splitting of the earliest human forms.[8] According to Aristophanes, attending to Eros is to respect the human need to find that which is most kindred to us, part of our lost ancient self. Socrates, on the other hand, presents an argument for a hierarchy of Eros in which sexual attraction is lowest and a platonic Eros, a spiritual love rooted in the pursuit of knowledge and wisdom, and marked by self-sacrifice and limitation—a disciplined eros—is at the top.[9] In the Socratic argument can be seen the preliminary of an erotic character of knowing and the mind/body dualism that haunts us still and was evident in my reading of *To Sir with Love*. As well, the entire mythology reverberates with connections that continue to pose theoretical challenges.

This mythology reveals the instability of a notion of eros, from its early mythic origins. In light of the preceding discussion, the evolution of the signifier *eros*—in its now dominant form, sexual desire—suggests, more a devolution, a narrowing and a lessening, in which the character of eros is eroded and delimited; this is in part an effect of the sexual repressions that characterize dominant western moral ideology.[10] As bell hooks (1994) argues, "[t]o understand the place of eros and eroticism in the classroom we must move beyond thinking of these forces solely in terms of the sexual, although that dimension need not be denied" (115). My intention here is to use the references to Greek mythology not only as context, but also as claim: the necessity of reclaiming more expanded multidimensional notions of eros. This expansion allows the project of eros, pedagogy, and the (re)negotiation of desire to be more usefully named, analyzed, and, itself, transformed. A revisiting of Greek mythology is only one source from which to seek direction for such expansion. Multiple notions of eros, expressed across diverse cultural fronts, enhance the complexity of erotic practices and their relationship to pedagogies.

Roger Simon (1992) begins his earlier brief discussion of eros and pedagogy with a reference to Jane Gallop and her analysis of the pederastic paradigm of classic Western teaching.[11] Simon's contention is that a pedagogy that is rooted in partiality, disruption, and the recognition of the embodiment of knowledge requires an eros that does not subvert "the desire to awake or incite a particular passion in those with whom we teach" (55) but which, rather, finds its expression in "the recognition of the particular dignity of others, not as objects, but as people with whom mutuality is possible" (72). Simon is very careful, however, neither to diminish nor to dismiss the dangers that attend dominant notions of pedagogy and that, too, invade radical pedagogies, however well intentioned or self-reflexive they may be.[12]

To represent this caveat more clearly, I again return to Greek and Roman mythology. Eros, in his dominant form, as Cupid, is invariably pictured with bow and arrow, poised to penetrate with desire. The traces of dominance, passivity, and objectification this image suggests for eros and pedagogy have not been sufficiently countered, despite the efforts of radical pedagogies to transform such relations of power. While it strikes me as necessary to reclaim eros, it is as necessary to reclaim it cautiously. Such caution demands, minimally, that we ask continuously of ourselves and our pedagogies what the sources of our passions and desires are, what effects our passions and desires have on others, and in what ways our passions and desires might interface with desiring others in productive and unproductive ways. I suggest it is our responses to these questions wherein lies the specificity of an erotic character of our pedagogies. For this reason alone, it is important to analyze responses to cultural texts of teaching as a means of locating a reflexive sense of personal eros and teaching.

■ Interrogating Eros

How might an interrogation of eros inform pedagogies that address the intersections of knowledge, power, and desire? The argument that language is the site and effect of desire was established in an earlier chapter (see Chapter 2). Following this argument, it may be that, to undercut dependency for need satisfaction, the search for meaning, for control of language and knowledge by the subject, is in some ways an enactment of the displacement of desire. If this is the case, then classrooms, as sites of knowledge production, signification, and representation (language practices), are necessarily implicated in the workings of desire. It may also be the case that pedagogies of uncertainty, which radical pedagogies are, may be less desirous for subjects positioned to know with more certainty and less ambivalence of the signifier. Radical pedagogies, while designed to address specific questions of knowledge, power, and desire, to be effective, must be also able to enact a "mobilization of desire" (Giroux 1994a, 278). It is my contention that to interrogate usefully the erotic character of pedagogy, it is necessary to address the social and psychic dynamics that may be at work in such mobilizations.

Eros, like desire, eludes rational grasp. To insist on an interrogation of eros is not to suggest that we can know fully its character. But it is possible to discern its patterns of signification. Indeed, the erotic character of pedagogy must, first and foremost, be recognized as a social and cultural practice of signification, historically specific and delimited by this specificity. A condition of desire, eros also eludes exactitude. Forged within social dynamics of difference and their associated differential distributions of power, its sources and expressions are also oftentimes, or in ways, more oppressive and oppressing than transformative. As subjects—teachers and students—we come to our classes already desiring, and bearing a history in which often deeply contradictory patterns of desire have already been established. I do not assume that these patterns are necessarily oppressive or oppressing; I do, however, contend that they oftentimes or in some ways are. As teachers, our pedagogies already hold a place of importance within our personal histories, and these pedagogies compete for a place within the histories of our students. It is in precisely this way that I understand Simon's point: "[A]s teachers with both vision and commitment, our relation to our students is part of a design we have on them. We do have images and ideas we think others should or could take seriously" (1992, 71). The erotic character of our pedagogies is enhanced when these visions and commitments, for whatever reasons, engage or map onto and enhance the dreams, desires, and fantasies of those positioned within our pedagogical discourses.

The challenge posed by this erotic character of pedagogy is twofold: how to respect difference; and, how to contend with the differentials of power that confront us in our pedagogies while, at the same time, insisting on the worth of our pedagogical projects. This challenge points to the unavoidable contradiction between mutuality (Simon 1992) and transformation precisely because, as I have pointed out, participants in transformative pedagogies are rarely on equitable footing. More specifically, then, this tension needs to be held as it urges a pondering of other difficult and pressing questions: In what directions can our passions and commitments be taken that are anti-invasive, yet rigorous, pleasurable, yet transformative? How might we envision a teaching that excites and incites, but in ways that facilitate the process of becoming the subjects of our own desires?

To begin to speculate on these questions, I return to an earlier point about eros as practice. Within poststructural pedagogies, any practice can be read as text, as signifying practice. That is, social practices can be interrogated for their structuring effects, the positions they offer subjects, the ways in which these positions are embedded in social relations of power, the effects of gaps, silences, omissions, and contradictions, and the place of the text in history in consort with or in opposition to other social/textual practices—in short, the productive and regulatory tendencies, for subjectivity, of social practices. Such work often is the curricular preoccupation of transformative pedagogies. Despite this preoccupation, however, easily eluded are the structuring effects, at the level of (dis)pleasure and desire, of the very pedagogies we use to deploy such concerns.

As necessary as it is to attend to texts that actively structure desire and work pedagogically, it is also necessary to attend to the constituting effects of these very *pedagogies as texts* themselves. As Deborah Britzman (1992) suggests, "to begin unravelling all that beckons us [as teachers and students] requires that we admit how we are implicated—or, how we take on, yet re-inflect—the intentions of others as if we were the author, not the bearer, of ideology" (168). Such reflexivity preempts a taken-for-grantedness that can accompany even radical pedagogies and that ignores the dynamics created by the very material conditions of classroom pedagogy: so much vested interest for so many diverse bodies in such a small social space. This taken-for-grantedness itself—the body confined—participates in the ongoing project of rationality, the severing of knowledge from the body and the unconscious. By ignoring its own indictment in formations of subjectivity, by default, pedagogies so characterized appear to stand apart from the murky grounds of desire and to beg a rationality they cannot sustain.

Approaching our own pedagogies as texts of desire, as texts constitutive of a material and discursive structuring of desiring bodies and psyches that (may or may not) favor a project of transformation is one way to resist such effects of disembodiment. That is, as well as seeing pedagogies of pleasure "out there" in, for example, the work of the popular or in dominant pedagogies, or advocating a pedagogy that addresses issues of desire, pleasure, and meaning, attention to eros and pedagogy involves a critique of the deployment of desire in the presentation of our own (pleasurable) pedagogical practices. My argument is not for a "will to pleasure" to replace former tyrannies, a "will to truth," or a "will to power," but, rather, is for a located, immediate, and present erotic politics, what bell hooks (1993) might call "a healing eroticism [found] in liberation struggle" (127).

The theoretical basis for a pedagogical model of eros can be found, in part, in Shoshana Felman's (1987) discussion of what she calls "the implication of psychoanalysis in pedagogy and of pedagogy in psychoanalysis" (75). In this oft-cited explanation, Felman draws on Lacan's work to explain how, in teaching (as in analysis), the pedagogue (the analyst) and the student (the analysand) are each students (and each pedagogues, for that matter) of knowledge as a structural dynamic dependent for its existence on mutuality. This dynamic is ideally effected through the (interminable) "transition, the struggle-filled passage" (89) to the realization that "[t]he subject of teaching is interminably—a student; the subject of teaching is interminably—a learning" (Felman 1987, 88). In this account, alterity is essential—the mutual embrace of the Other, "the place of the signifier" (Coward and Ellis 1977, 109), who can teach us what it is we know and the unconscious structuring of that knowing.

The "struggle-filled passage" to which Felman refers is the point on which I wish to focus. Felman stops short of confronting the alienation, itself interminable, of subjects as a consequence of the inequitable character of the various dimensions of the symbolic order. As I have mentioned earlier, in relation to my own teaching, teachers can and oftentimes do become major characters in the emotive dynamics of pedagogy. This dynamic, *transference*, originates in the work of Freud and refers to "the compulsive unconscious reproduction of an archaic emotional pattern" (Felman 1987, 85). In his rereading of Freud, Jacques Lacan claims that transference is an inevitable character of teaching, one synonymous with relating to authority and the illusion of what Lacan called "the subject presumed to know" (Felman 1987, 85–6). Transference, then, can be seen as a potentially positive as well as a necessary dynamic, in psychoanalysis and pedagogy. Felman, following Lacan, locates the basis of teaching as "an emotional, erotic experience" (86) in transference. The signifying field of this eroticism can be the urgency and pleasure of the production of knowledge.

As other writers (Simon 1992; hooks 1994) also point out, such an eroticism is deepened by the concomitant building of community and transformative social vision. In radical pedagogies, in pedagogies deliberately designed to disrupt, the instability of the subject can and often is enhanced. In such cases, recast desire, i.e., transference, provides an anchoring effect. One way in which this phenomenon is displayed is in the expressed feelings by students, for example, that the pedagogue knows and can empathize with, the difficulties of occupying marginalized discourses. Overacceptance of or overreliance on such dynamics intensifies transference. Redirecting such desires to the broader community of change is one way in which the intensification of transference can be contained. The political usefulness of transference can thus be seen; the building of community is enhanced by the healthy containment of a necessary dynamic. Failure to contain transference, then, can be seen as both personally and educationally detrimental and politically ineffective.

Transference, as any other practice, is culturally bound and never occurs outside determining, if not deterministic, relations of power. Unsurprisingly, then, the teacher, the one in whom the illusion of the subject presumed to know is most likely or most often invested, even within radical pedagogies, can become akin to what Joanne Pagano (1994) calls the "professor of desire" (255). Within Pagano's configuration, students identify the teacher as the locus of desire and take on as their own the desires of the teacher, and it is in the teacher's likeness that students are recreated both to receive and to execute the passions of the one presumed to know. As Pagano points out, this dynamic, borne as much out of the desires of the professor as those of the student—in other words, as much a condition of countertransference as of transference—is a disturbing and dangerous one, particularly for women and Others whose position within the social order is constituted negatively and against the odds of attaining greater control over the process of signification. Pagano's warnings heighten my argument for a constant reflexivity toward the workings of desire within and through our pedagogies. Within radical pedagogies, then, the pitfalls of dependency and power that can accompany transference/countertransference require demystification, diffusion, and resistance.

Within radical pedagogies, it seems especially pressing to address these issues, not only because the personal and partial conditions of knowledge construction are named explicitly and critiqued ungoingly, but also because such relationships are at the heart of questions of pedagogy and power. Any pretence of egalitarianism of relationship, while sometimes propagated from the political naiveté (or denial) of liberal humanism disguised as radicalism, is unacceptable in such contexts.

Madeleine Grumet (1988) says of the pretence of "mutuality of egalitarianism" (115):

> That mutuality, for all its romanticism, fails the pedagogical project in three respects. First, like the fascination of lovers, it is blind to the world, making the other's look the end rather than the means in the act of knowing. Second, this stance is dishonest, for it denies the asymmetry in the student/teacher relation. It disclaims the teacher's power, in the world and in the institution, and in so doing prohibits the student from deconstructing and appropriating the perspective of the teacher's look for his or her own vision. Third, the ideal of equality fosters an eroticism that ensnares both teacher and student in their reciprocal gaze. (115)

What Grumet's comments point to is the difficulty of containment of transference where the politics of pedagogical relationships are denied or ignored.

Clearly, then, the conditions of mutuality and community-building that accompany radical pedagogies, the isolating, alienating environments in which radical pedagogues often work, and the disruption and alienation often created by the adoption by students of marginalized discourses can make "achieving the right distance" (Taubman 1992, 216) a more nuanced and knotty condition. At a minimum a clear, reflexive sense of the structuring of our own desires through knowledge, power, and pedagogy and a persistent monitoring of the impact of our pedagogies in the mobilization of desire and/in others are required. Such reflexivity is proposed not as a means of denying the possibility of healthy, empowering relationships or, for that matter, the agency and/or complex subjectivities of all participants in pedagogy (hooks 1995). It is difficult to contain transference if one denies or does not reflect on its ongoing dynamics. Transference is one site where the possible shadows of an erotic character of pedagogy—those aspects of our eroticism that encompass "what is most narcissistic and most imperialistic in our relation to the world" (Gallop 1988, 157)—can show themselves. More hopeful passions emerge from seeking to understand the constitutive shape and texture of those shadows.

As I implied in my earlier example, moving toward more hopeful passions requires, in part, a moving away from and/or beyond, without necessarily abandoning, the more singular personal dynamics of pedagogy. Ultimately, the project of radical pedagogies is a collective project attuned to the political dimensions of the personal as the intimate site of the workings of the social. Uncontained transference/countertransference diverts energy from political passions onto individuals (Belsey 1985, 54), the antithesis of the project of radical pedagogies. Despite its liberal humanist inclinations and its cultural limitations, psychoanalysis can provide important insights into and possible directions from which to explore further the dynamics that inform and further sociopolitical projects. It is increasingly obvious that this connection between the psychic and the social is part of what is instrumental to such a pedagogy of desire.

■ Closing Cautions

Since we cannot put on new bodies before we desocialize our old ones, the task at hand requires us to provide the mediative ground for a refleshed corporeality. This means the creation of embodied knowledges that can help us refigure the lineaments of our desires and chart the path towards the realization of our collective needs outside and beyond the suffocating constraints of capital and patriarchy.

—Peter McLaren (1995, 64–5)

The preceding discussion of eros and pedagogy located the problematic in both hopeful and hazardous terms. As a culminating discussion of desire-in-practice, it, in many ways, urges a revisit of many of the issues raised in previous chapters. For example, the issues developed earlier around a discussion of *Exotica* (see Chapter 5), in particular those related to gaze and subjectivity, are relevant. The teacher's gaze as it is employed in many classrooms, and as Madeleine Grumet (1988) points out, is "a strategy of domination" (111). Eroticized, such a gaze has disturbing political parameters. Several educators (Grumet 1988; Pagano 1991) suggest the complications of auto/biographical work and eros. Still others address the intricate politics of eros and difference (hooks 1992).

Still other questions remain. For example, does the signifier *eros* adequately capture the emotive dynamics of a caring, passionate, desiring, and pleasurable pedagogy? Given how traditional discourses of eros and pleasure inscribe subjects within phallocentric, heterosexist positions, how might current practices of eros and pedagogy contain or counter such positionings? The performative function of eros cannot avoid its present limits; however, neither must it relinquish its history or its horizons to the present. The discursive struggle over naming what I and others are, for now, at least, content to call an erotic character of pedagogy is an ongoing one. The performative differences will be

felt in the resistances to and affirmations of such naming and in the disquieting yet hopeful turns such naming can release into struggle. The
limited discourses of psychoanalysis, mythology, and pedagogy, out of
which, in this paper, the configurations of eros and desire are derived,
point to grounds for contestation already well established and ongoing.

An erotic character of pedagogy that is in keeping with a socially
transformative project aims to break, not reproduce, the nexus between
pleasure and powerlessness. As persons responsible for our pedagogies,
the design we might have on our students should not be driven by the
desire to recruit them into our own commitments. As teachers whose
desires can have a certain authority in students' lives, it seems necessary
to reassert the grounds for becoming desiring subjects, the subjects of
our own desires who desire with and against one another. While pedagogy is always practiced as a form of persuasion (Giroux and Simon
1989, 14), a self-cautiousness should exist that attempts to counter
inclinations that might usurp the dignity of desiring others with whom
we engage on the grounds of (dis)pleasure and difference.

Yet, such cautions should be measured as we veer away from, and not
toward, still other perils. Ultraconservative voices would prefer to quell
the discussion of desire and pedagogy, or else, coopt its terms to fascist
ends. This point is not an attempt at alarmism; history is replete with
catastrophic examples of the manipulations of desire through horrific
means and to irreparable ends—pedagogy at its most vile. As well, there
is the tendency toward what Valerie Walkerdine (1990) calls "embour-
geoisement" (202), the intellectualization of desire, pleasure, and passion as regulatory and in service of current hegemonies, and through
which tendencies the discussions of an erotic character of pedagogy
could threaten the constituting grounds of desire of those subjects
deemed "Other." To maintain a respectful sense of the body (the subject) as the target of pedagogy and to tap the utopian inclinations of
eros are real challenges for a radical pedagogy that commits to naming
its desires.

▪

Finally, wherein lie such possibilities of transgression and hope? The
precise location of hope within an erotic character of pedagogy is in the
use of that energy to promote collective good. Contemporary psychoanalysis and radical pedagogies must confer more deeply to engage in
an intensification of the mutually informing project of defining the psychic and social terrain of enhanced possibility. There is much evidence

of the ineffectiveness of the denial of the implication of pleasure and desire in pedagogy, of the pedagogical condemnation of certain forms of desire—for example, those expressed through the popular—and of the uninterrogated celebration of some forms of desire—for example, "the rosy 'eroticism' of all-female teaching" (Gallop 1995, 81). There is less evidence with which to determine more fully the possibilities of pedagogies that allow us to become more intimate with the structuring of our own desires, including those mobilized within our pedagogies. In this respect, it is essential that pedagogy as cultural practices aimed at the (re)design and (re)negotiation of desire on the site of the subject is recognized—the work of resignifying as eros-bearing, material, and embodied. Teaching as "disturbing pleasures" (Giroux 1994), indeed!

■ Notes

■ Chapter One

1. I use the term *postmodern* to suggest a series of social and cultural conditions; I use the term *poststructural* to name the analytic traditions that constitute a rewriting of structuralist thought. Many aspects of poststructural critique have been appropriated and expanded by theorists whose writings are increasingly named as postmodern, writings that express a concern with and a critique of the totalizing tendencies of modernist thought. Often, such writings make no reference to poststructural theories, per se. Still for all, the two are, in ways, obviously and fruitfully compatible. Some writers interchange the two signifiers. I, however, resist the tendency to interchange in order to avoid the collapse of signifiers. See Figure 1.1, at the end of the chapter, for further explication of similarities and distinctions between postmodern and poststructural.

2. The writings of Matthew Arnold, the nineteenth-century English poet and critic, and F.R. Leavis, the early-twentieth-century English critic, had a profound impact on the dominant definitions of English Studies, in particular, that of the discourse of cultural literacy.

3. Critical educators have also made important arguments for the necessity of incorporating the insights of critical pedagogy into cultural studies. See, for example, H.A. Giroux (1994), *Disturbing Pleasures* and L. Grossberg (1994), "Bringin' It All Back Home—Pedagogy and Cultural Studies," in H. A. Giroux and P. McLaren, eds., *Between Borders: Pedagogy and the Politics of Cultural Studies.*

4. I use the umbrella term "radical pedagogies" as a reference that includes critical pedagogy, feminist pedagogy, antiracist and anticolonialist pedagogy, and antidiscriminatory pedagogy. My intention is not to collapse these pedagogies and their often competing agendas. Rather, my intention is to create a common reference point for forms of pedagogical practice more overtly and radically political, out of which many of the insights to which I refer come and/or to which they attend.

5. For examples of further discussion of popular culture and critical peda-

gogy, see Henry Giroux (1994), *Disturbing Pleasures* and Henry Giroux, Roger Simon, et al. (1989), *Popular Culture, Schooling, and Everyday Life*.

6. For an excellent discussion of this relationship, see Chapter 4, "Psychoanalysis and Education: Teaching Terminable and Interminable" in Shoshana Felman (1987), *Jacques Lacan and the Adventure of Insight: Psychoanalysis in Contemporary Culture*.

■ Chapter Two

1. The term *language* here references all signifying practices, those means by which meaning is encoded and communicated. In this sense, words are but one way in which meaning is "sign-ed" or in which language is mobilized; movement, objects, images, etcetera, are others. See David Graddol (1994), "Three Models of Language Description" for a further explanation of this "postmodern model of language."

2. The phrase "the incarnation of desire" is taken from Margaret Atwood (1993), *The Robber Bride* p.31.

3. For a particularly insightful discussion of the discursivity of the body, sex, and gender, see Judith Butler (1993), *Bodies That Matter: On the Discursive Limits of "Sex."*

4. Certainly, poststructural notions of language can lend themselves to a distancing, a technicism that can ignore the person in the subject position(s) of a discourse in favor of attention to the intertextual workings of discourse itself. For a useful critique of such poststructural theory, see Gregory Jay (1995), "Taking Multiculturalism Personally: Ethnos and Ethos in the Classroom," in Jane Gallop, ed., *Pedagogy: The Question of Impersonation*

5. For examples of work that manifests these rationalist leanings, see Pamela Gilbert and Sandra Taylor (1991), *Fashioning the Feminine: Girls, Popular Culture and Schooling*. Such work, while emphasizing the importance of the cultural sphere and its design on feminine subjectivities, downplays the difficult (re)negotiations of desire entailed in such "refashioning of the feminine."

6. While I accept the feminist critiques of Lacan, I do believe, as do many feminists, that it is possible to take advantage of some of his insights—in particular, those that relate to the issue at hand, the structuring of desire in language—to raise important questions concerning the intersections of subjectivity, knowledge and power.

7. For a clear discussion of semiotics and, in particular, how it relates to psychoanalysis, see Kaja Silverman (1983), *The Subject of Semiotics*.

8. This feeling I now understand as a form of silence, the effect of sediments of invalidation, perhaps experienced when I did *have words for it*. I repressed the causes but not the feelings that were their effects. I located the problem in language, rather than in the cultural effects, felt personally, of language use. In other words, the structure of listening was also a factor in the feelings I experienced. I thank Pat Singer for helping me reach this insight.

9. Roger Simon (1992) has written insightfully about the basis of such student experiences in the chapter, "The Fear of Theory," in *Teaching Against the Grain*.

10. In her introduction to *Thinking Through the Body*, Jane Gallop (1988) uses the metaphor of decapitation to describe the mind-body split (1) and that of strangulation to describe the prevention of "the life giving flow between the two" (5).

11. The "inside" responses to the collection of articles in *Feminisms and Critical Pedagogy* (1992), edited by Carmen Luke and Jennifer Gore, and Gore's *The Struggle for Pedagogies* (1993) galvanize this point.

12. For a discussion of the political efficacy of certain notions of home and homelessness, see Henry Giroux (1994), "Paulo Freire and the Rise of the Border Intellectual" in his *Disturbing Pleasures*.

13. Some of the comments in this section are included in a shorter piece. See S. Church, J. Portelli, C. MacInnis, A. Vibert, and U. Kelly (1995), "Reconsidering Whole Language: Five Perspectives," *English Quarterly* 27: 1/2, 5–14.

14. The term *whole language* is used here to refer to language practices that share common characteristics. In the literature, the terms *whole language, natural language, progressive literacy, new literacy, response-based literacy*, and *growth model literacy* capture similar practices as they relate to the discussion here. My intent is not to conflate these movements but rather to point to general characteristics they share.

15. For my purposes here, liberal humanism is defined briefly as those beliefs, which Catherine Belsey (1985) calls "the consensual orthodoxy of the west" (ix), that center the individual and the rights, liberties, and freedoms attendant on the individual in an (idealized) democratic society. Of particular concern here is the assumption within liberalism of the stable, unified, human subject whose essential "human nature" is unchangeable.

■ Chapter Three

1. I use the term *auto/biography* to refer to any self-referential writing, i.e., journals, diaries, stories, etc., that presents explicit and peculiar links of experience, identity, and consciousness in the name of a signed author. I acknowledge the term as somewhat of a misnomer given poststructural theoretical insights, which throw into question the extent to which it is possible to claim to write one's life within discursive contexts into which subjects are already written. I have used a slash to separate the prefix *auto* from *biography* to signal a poststructural break of the happy union of self (*auto*) and story (*biography*). This break also marks the alienation of self-in-language.

2. For a concise overview of autobiography in education, see Robert Graham (1991), *Reading and Writing the Self: Autobiography in Education and the Curriculum*.

3. An example is the collection of essays edited by Carol Witherell and Nel Noddings (1991), *Stories Lives Tell: Narrative and Dialogue in Education*.

4. As John Willinsky (1994) notes, postcolonialism, "[w]hile certainly indebted to such leading poststructuralists as Foucault and Derrida . . . has a more certain intellectual and political agenda . . . " (615) than either postmodernism, with its critique of meta-narratives, and poststructuralism, with its indeterminacy of meaning.

5. For a useful discussion of the politics of popular representations of innocence and nostalgia, see Henry Giroux (1994), "Politics and Innocence in the Wonderful World of Disney" (25–45) in his *Disturbing Pleasures*.

6. For an exceptional analysis of witnessing, see Shoshana Felman and Dori Laub (1992), *Testimony: Crises of Witnessing in Literature, Psychoanalysis, and History*.

7. This notion of coming to my story through the story of another (an Other) is brilliantly developed by Shoshana Felman (1993), *What Does a Woman Want: Reading and Sexual Difference*.

8. For a discussion of the complexities of silence, confession and historical responsibility in relation, with specific reference to the case of de Man, see Shoshana Felman (1992), "After the Apocalypse: Paul de Man and the Fall to Silence." In Shoshana Felman and Dori Laub, *Testimony: Crises of Witnessing in Literature, Psychoanalysis and History* (120–164).

9. I first read Valerie Walkerdine's "Dreams from an Ordinary Childhood" in 1986. This courageous and insightful autobiography not only touched me deeply but also urged a revisiting of my own childhood pictures. See Valerie Walkerdine (1990), *School Girl Fictions* for an effective interweaving of theory, autobiography, culture, and pedagogy.

10. Attempting to maintain this dialectic is a common feature of radical pedagogies that begin from the partial, constitutive, and mutual conditions of knowing. For a useful consideration of the psychoanalytic (Lacanian) complexities of one aspect of such a dialectic for teachers, see Peter Taubman (1992), "Achieving the Right Distance." In W.F. Pinar and W.M. Reynolds, eds., *Understanding Curriculum as Phenomenological and Deconstructed Text*.

11. For a discussion of how the look dominates classrooms, see Madeleine Grumet (1988), "My Face in Thine Eyes, Thine in Mine Appears: The Look in Parenting and Pedagogy," in her *Bitter Milk: Women and Teaching*.

■ Chapter Four

1. The phrase *popular culture*, as I use it here, is meant to signify certain differences from the related terms, *mass media* and *mass culture*. *Popular* signals more than currency and mass; it evokes a counter-practice and a politics of pleasure. *Culture* signals the social relations of which the popular is representative and constitutive. *Mass*, on the other hand, signals patterns of production, dis-

tribution, and consumption; *media*, likewise, signals the technologies through which culture is encoded and dispensed. My own concern with the politics of pleasure and desire and their cultural effects is best captured in *popular culture*.

2. For a clear and succinct articulation of the postmodern and its implications for literacy education and English Studies, see James Berlin (1993), "Literacy, Pedagogy, and English Studies: Postmodern Connections."

3. Thorough and insightful essays on the legacies and directions of cultural studies can be found in David Morley and Kuan-Hsing Chen, eds., (1996) *Stuart Hall: Critical Dialogues in Cultural Studies*, and Angela McRobbie (1994), *Postmodernism and Popular Culture*. Richard Johnson (1983), "What Is Cultural Studies Anyway?" *Anglistica* 26: 1–2 is also a useful piece.

4. Important arguments for the relationship of cultural studies and critical pedagogy are offered by Henry Giroux (1994), in *Disturbing Pleasures* and the several essays in Giroux (1994), *Between Borders: Pedagogy and the Politics of Cultural Studies*.

5. For an extensive analysis of the implications of importing the terminology of literary study into the broader practices of cultural studies, see Robert Morgan (1993), "Transitions from English to Cultural Studies," *Curriculum & Teaching* 8: 1, 103–130.

6. Such ideologically overt naming of the dominant presuppositions that inform the version of English on offer here is never critiqued within the document, despite its assertion that "critical literacy" is a curricular goal.

7. Of note here are examples from the makers of computer hardware and software who utilize the educational rhetoric of empowerment to reduce knowledge, power, and democracy to technological gymnastics, accessibility, and mouse-tip interfacing while simultaneously promoting a rigid bureaucratic ethic of technicism and efficiency.

■ Chapter Five

The phrase "the dream's malfunction" is taken from "Song for Sharon" by Joni Mitchell, recorded on *Hejira* (Elektra Entertainment, 1976).

1. *Exotica* won the 1994 International Critics Award at the Cannes Film Festival and was awarded eight Canadian Genie Awards, including Best Picture, Best Director, and Best Screenplay.

2. It is of some interest that Egoyan's film was made and released at a time in Canada when three trials concerning schoolgirl murders dominated the media: the Homolka-Bernardo trials for the murders of Leslie Mahaffey and Kristin French; and the false conviction and subsequent acquittal of Guy Morin for the murder of Christine Jessop. While even the names of the schoolgirls in *Exotica* —Lisa and Christina—recall the victims of these crimes (just as the uniform recalls widely circulated pictures of the victims), the trials themselves are part of a larger context of a North American debate about, on the one

hand, the treatment of sex offenders, whose victims are largely female, and the conduct of media, on the other. Egoyan's film raises questions related to both these issues.

3. Alice Munro (1971), *Lives of Girls and Women*.

4. For a discussion of the contradictions created for female adolescents who are positioned with specific and conflicting discourses of femininity, see Sandra Taylor (1993), "Transforming the Texts: Towards a Feminist Classroom Practice" in K. Christian-Smith, ed., *Texts of Desire: Essays on Fiction, Femininity, and Schooling*.

■ Chapter Six

1. I am using the term "colonized" to indicate the historical subject formed under the conditions of empire, particularly through the processes of domination, erasure through assimilation, and racialization, whose legacy and experiences are the embodiment of colonization.

2. I refer to the range of decentering theoretical discourses—postmodernism, poststructuralism, posthumanism, post-Fordism, postfeminism, etc.—which attempt to redefine the subject under radically altered social and historical circumstances.

3. The largely French province of Quebec has struggled since the Canadian Confederation in 1867 with its minority status within Canada. Two referendums designed to bring to bear a democratic vote on separation from Canada, one in 1982 and another in 1995, have resulted in a decision to remain a province of Canada. In the 1995 campaign, the "minority vote," seen to be more allied with English interests in Quebec, was a focus of the lobby for separation.

4. For a biting critique of such a model, see Jamaica Kincaid's *A Small Place*. Kincaid presents the ravages of (internalized) colonialism of her island of birth, Antigua, which is a current, accessible, and provocative example of co-implication.

5. Richard Rodriguez is the author of *Hunger of Memory: The Education of Richard Rodriguez* (1982), an autobiography which addresses the dynamics of education and cultural assimilation.

6. For a rigorous and insightful analysis of Benetton, see chapter 1 of Henry Giroux (1994), *Disturbing Pleasures*.

7. The measure of difficulty—from a perspective of racialized difference—such interventions of identity in pedagogy can create is seen in Cheryl Johnson (1995), "Disinfecting Dialogues." In Jane Gallop, ed., *Pedagogy: The Question of Impersonation*. Johnson discusses her rejection of the personal in pedagogy as the necessary cost of protectionism in a racist and sexist environment

■ Chapter Seven

I thank Susan Gannett for her detailed comments on an earlier version of this chapter.

1. I derive the phrase "passion designs" from a conflation of ideas expressed by Roger Simon (1992) in his discussion of eros and pedagogy. Simon speaks of "the desire to incite a particular passion in those whom we teach" (55), and that "[a]s teachers with both vision and commitment, our relation to our students is part of a design we have on them. We do have images and ideas we think others should or could usefully take seriously" (71).

2. Indeed, some of this dynamic of repression manifested itself in my response and the responses of others to my decision to write about eros and teaching. While many recognized the importance of such discussions, some with whom I shared my initial interest in this topic responded with what struck me as a mild form of titillation thinly disguised as intrigue. Others questioned why I needed to use "those words"—eros and desire, in particular. As for myself, I marked my self-consciousness around the topic and noted even a defensiveness when responding to questions of interest. I note these responses because I think they demonstrate part of this dynamic as an effect of at least two things: the dominant association of eros with a form of sexual energy only; and the internalization (by women, in particular, and myself included) of feelings of shame, negativity, and guilt around not just sexuality but forms of passion, generally.

3. Nor is it my intention to reduce these examples to the singular theme of eros and teaching. Rather, my point is that this theme is present, in varying degrees, for differing purposes and with differing effects, within each of these examples.

4. The sequel, *To Sir with Love II*, was released in 1996. In this film, an older Thackeray returns to America where, having lost none of his polish and effectiveness, he is able to convert the anger of a cast of Chicago inner-city school youth.

5. The source of identification, as an adult, has shifted. In recent viewings of the film, I more easily identify with the students, in particular with Denim's expressions of anger. As well, a degree of pathos accompanies my engagement of Thackeray. I attribute this difference not only to the restructuring of my own desires, discursively, over time, but to a belief that my failure to identify with any of the students and my over-identification with Thackeray were each forms of refusals. It is my sense that there was too much at stake for me, as an adolescent viewing the film, to allow for a safe identification with the working-class students in the film.

6. I use Sally Munt's term here because it captures best for me the gist of the stories students relate to me about what they see to be the positive impact of our classroom experiences. I do not wish to claim a place in these narratives as the major player; rather, I am attempting to summarize what students identify as my place in a larger dynamic in which my own passion, commitment, and vision do have an impact.

7. My references for this discussion of Greek and Roman mythology include *The Encyclopedia of Myths and Legends of all Nations* (1950) by H.S.

Robinson and K. Wilson; the second edition of *Classical Mythology* (1997) by M.P.O. Morford and R. J. Lenardon; *The Greek Myths* (1959) by Robert Graves; and *Bulfinch's Mythology* (1979) compiled by B. Holme.

8. The myth evoked by Aristophanes is that of a three-sexed humanity— male, female, and androgynous—who threatened the gods. The gods responded by weakening rather than killing the humans by physically splitting each one, thereby leaving the parts longing for the whole. This myth explained heterosexuality (the split androgyne pursuing its missing half), male homosexuality (the split male pursuing its missing half), and lesbianism (the split female pursuing its missing half). Eros, in this scenario, is the force that prompts the pursuit of wholeness.

9. To demonstrate his argument, Socrates draws on a conversation with a woman named Diotima who tells him of the conception of Eros by Resourcefulness and Poverty, parentage that ensures Eros has a character marked by ingenuity, need, and desire. Cast in a state between desire and wisdom, Eros loves wisdom as a symptom of his own lack and as the highest form of his own fulfillment.

10. I would argue that any notion of eros that delimits or eliminates any dimensions of a constructive expression of human passion is devolutionary. In other words, it is not my intention to equate devolution and lessening with sexual eros only.

11. The discussion of pedagogy in this light is found in Jane Gallop (1982), "The Immoral Teachers."

12. For a more extended discussion by Simon of eros and pedagogy, see R.I. Simon (1995), "Face to Face with Alterity: Postmodern Jewish Identity and the Eros of Pedagogy." In J. Gallop, ed., *Pedagogy: The Question of Impersonation.*

■ References

■ Atwood, M. (1993). *The Robber Bride*. Toronto: McClelland and Stewart.

Ball, S., Kenny, A., and Gardiner, D. (1990). Literacy, Politics, and the Teaching of English. In I. Goodson and P. Medway, eds., *Bringing English to Order*, 47–86. London: Falmer Press.

Barthes, R. (1979). From Work to Text. In J.V. Harari, ed., *Textual Strategies: Perspectives in Post-Structuralist Criticism*, 73–81. Ithaca: Cornell University Press.

Belsey, C. (1980). *Critical Practice*. London: Methuen.

———. (1985). *The Subject of Tragedy: Identity and Difference in Renaissance Drama*. London: Methuen.

Bennison, S. and Porteous, J. (1989). "I See the Murderer Is a Skilful Door Opener": Investigating Autobiography and Detective Stories with 11-to 18-Year-Olds. In P. Brooker and P. Humm, eds., *Dialogue and Difference: English Into the Nineties*, 171–184. London: Routledge.

Berlin, J. (1993). Literacy, Pedagogy, and English Studies: Postmodern Connections. In C. Lankshear and P. McLaren, eds., *Critical Literacy: Politics, Praxis, and the Postmodern Turn*, 247–269. Albany: SUNY Press.

Bernstein, N. (1995, March-April). Goin' Gangstra, Choosin' Cholita. *UTNE Reader* 68: 87–90.

Bhabha, H. (1990). DissemiNation: Time, Narrative, and the Margins of the Modern Nation. In H. Bhabha, ed., *Nation and Narration*, 291–322. New York: Routledge.

Brady, J. and Hernandez, A. (1993). Feminist Literacies: Toward Emancipatory Possibilities of Solidarity. In C. Lankshear and P. McLaren, eds., *Critical Literacy: Politics, Praxis, and the Postmodern*, 323–334. Albany: SUNY Press.

Britzman, D. (1992). Decentring Discourses in Teacher Education: Or, the Unleashing of Unpopular Things. In K. Weiler and C. Mitchell, eds., *What Schools Can Do: Critical Pedagogy and Practice*, 151–175. Albany: SUNY Press.

Brossard, N. (1990). *Mauve Desert* (S. de Lotbiniere-Harwood, trans.). Toronto: Coach House Press. (Original work published 1987.)

Bryson, M. and de Castell, S. (1995). So We've Got a Chip on our Shoulders: Sexing the Texts of "Educational Technology." In J. Gaskell and J. Willinsky, eds., *Gender In/Forms Curriculum: From Enrichment to Transformation*, 21–42. New York: Teachers College Press.

Buckingham, D. and Sefton-Green, J. (1994). *Cultural Studies Goes To School: Reading and Teaching Popular Media*. London: Taylor & Francis.

Butler, J. (1993). *Bodies That Matter: On the Discursive Limits of "Sex."* New York: Routledge.

———. (1990). *Gender Trouble: Feminism and the Subversion of Identity*. New York: Routledge.

Cherland, M.R. and Edelsky, C. (1993). Girls and Reading: The Desire for Agency and the Horror of Helplessness in Fictional Encounters. In L.K. Christian-Smith, ed., *Texts of Desire*, 28–44. London: Falmer Press.

Christian-Smith, L.K. (1990). *Becoming a Woman Through Romance*. London: Routledge.

———, ed. (1993). *Texts of Desire: Essays on Fiction, Femininity, and Schooling*. London: Falmer Press.

Christie, F. (1993). The "Received Tradition" of English Teaching: The Decline of Rhetoric and the Corruption of Grammar. In B. Green, ed., *The Insistence of the Letter: Literacy Studies and Curriculum Theorizing*, 75–106. Pittsburg: University of Pittsburg Press.

Church, S., Portelli, J., MacInnis, C., Vibert, A., and Kelly, U. (1995). Reconsidering Whole Language: Five Perspectives. *The English Quarterly* 27: 1–2, 5–14.

Clavell, J., producer & director. 1966. *To Sir With Love* [film]. Burbank, CA: Columbia Pictures.

Corrigan, P. (1988). The Making of the Boy: Mediations on What Grammar School Did With, To, and For My Body. *Journal of Education* 170: 3, 142–161.

———. (1983/4). "My" Body, My "Self"? Trying to See My Masculine Eyes. *Resources for Feminist Research* 12: 4, 29–32.

Coward, R. (1985). *Female Desires: How They Are Sought, Bought, and Packaged*. New York: Grove Press.

———, and Ellis, J. (1977). *Language and Materialism: Developments in Semiology and the Theory of the Subject*. London: Routledge & Kegan Paul.

Davies, B. (1993). Beyond Dualisms and Towards Multiple Subjectivities. In L.K. Christian-Smith, ed., *Texts of Desire: Essays on Fiction, Femininity and Schooling*, 145–173. London: Falmer Press.

———. (1990). The Problem of Desire. *Social Problems* 37: 4, 801–816.

Delpit, L. (1988). The Silenced Dialogue: Power and Pedagogy in Educating Other People's Children. *Harvard Educational Review* 58: 3, 280–298.

Dyson, M.E. (1993). *Reflecting Black: African-American Cultural Criticism*. Minneapolis: University of Minnesota Press.

———. (1994). Be like Mike? Michael Jordan and the Pedagogy of Desire. In

H.A. Giroux and P. McLaren, eds., *Between Borders: Pedagogy and the Politics of Cultural Studies*, 119–126. New York: Routledge.

Ebert, T.L. (1991). The "Difference" of Postmodern Feminism. *College English* 53: 8, 886–904.

Egoyan, A., producer director. 1994. *Exotica* [film]. Toronto: Ego Film Arts Production.

Ellsworth, E. (1992, Fall). Teaching to Support Unassimilated Difference. *Radical Teacher* 42, 4–9.

Fagan, C. (1995, March 25). Poets Three: Stillness in Borson, Action with Moure, Glosas with Page. *Globe and Mail*, C7.

Felman, S. (1987). *Jacques Lacan and the Adventure of Insight: Psychoanalysis in Contemporary Culture*. Cambridge, MA: Harvard University Press.

———. (1993). *What Does a Woman Want? Reading and Sexual Difference*. Baltimore: Johns Hopkins.

———, and Laub, D. (1992). *Testimony: Crises of Witnessing in Literature, Psychoanalysis, and History*. New York: Routledge.

Ferdman, B.M. (1990). Literacy and Cultural Identity. *Harvard Educational Review* 60: 2, 181–204.

Fine, M. (1992). *Disruptive Voices: The Possibilities of Feminist Research*. Ann Arbor: University of Michigan Press.

Foundation for the Atlantic Canada English Language Arts Curriculum. (1995). Halifax: Department of Education and Culture, Government of Nova Scotia.

Freire, P. and Macedo, D. *Literacy: Reading the Word and the World*. South Hadley: Bergin & Garvey.

Gallop, J. (1982). The Immoral Teachers. *Yale French Studies* 62, 117–128.

———. (1988). *Thinking Through the Body*. New York: Columbia University Press.

———. (1995). Im-Personation: A Reading in the Guise of an Introduction. In J. Gallop, ed., *Pedagogy: The Question of Impersonation*, 1–18. Bloomington: Indiana University Press.

Gates, Jr., H.L. (1985). Writing "Race" and the Difference It Makes. In H.L. Gates, Jr., ed., *"Race", Writing, and Difference*. Chicago: University of Chicago Press.

Gilbert, P. (1991). From Voice to Text: Reconsidering Writing and Reading in the English Classroom. *English Education* 24: 4, 195–211.

———, and Taylor, S. (1991). *Fashioning the Feminine*. Sydney: Allen & Unwin.

Giroux, H.A. (1990). *Curriculum Discourse as Postmodernist Critical Practice*. Geelong, Australia: Deakin University Press.

———. (1994). *Disturbing Pleasures: Learning Popular Culture*. New York: Routledge.

———. (1994a). Doing Cultural Studies: Youth and the Challenge of Pedagogy. *Harvard Educational Review* 64: 3, 278–308.

———. (1993). Literacy and the Politics of Difference. In C. Lankshear and P.

McLaren, eds., *Critical Literacy: Politics, Praxis and the Postmodern*, 367–377. Albany: SUNY Press.

————, and Simon, R.I. (1989). Popular Culture as a Pedagogy of Pleasure and Meaning. In H.A. Giroux, R.I. Simon, and Contributors, *Popular Culture, Schooling, and Everyday Life*, 1–29. Toronto: OISE Press.

Golsan, R. (1995, November–December). Fashionable Fascism. *UTNE Reader* 72, 60.

Gore, J. (1993). *The Struggle for Pedagogies: Critical and Feminist Discourses as Regimes of Truth*. New York: Routledge.

Gotfrit, L. (1991). Women Dancing Back: Disruption and the Politics of Pleasure. In H.A. Giroux, ed., *Postmodernism, Feminism, and Cultural Politics: Redrawing Educational Boundaries*, 174–195. Albany: SUNY Press.

Graddol, D. (1994). Three Models of Language Description. In D. Graddol and O. Boyd-Barrett, eds., *Media Texts: Authors and Readers*, 1–21. Philadelphia: The Open University.

Graham, R.J. (1991). *Reading and Writing the Self: Autobiography in Education and the Curriculum*. New York: Teachers College Press.

Graves, R. (1959). *The Greek Myths: Vol. 1*. New York: George Braziller, Inc.

Green, B. (1990). A Dividing Practice: "Literature," English Teaching, and Cultural Politics. In I. Goodson and P. Medway, eds., *Bringing English to Order*, 135–161. London: Falmer Press.

————. (1993). Literacy Studies and Curriculum Theorizing; or, the Insistence of the Letter. In B. Green, ed., *The Insistence of the Letter: Literacy Studies and Curriculum Theorizing*, 195–225. Pittsburg: University of Pittsburg Press.

Grossberg, L. (1994). Bringin' It All Back Home—Pedagogy and Cultural Studies. In H.A. Giroux and P. McLaren, eds., *Between Borders: Pedagogy and the Politics of Cultural Studies*, 1–25. New York: Routledge.

Grumet, M. (1995). Scholae Personae: Masks for Meaning. In J. Gallop, ed., *Pedagogy: The Question of Impersonation*, 36–45. Bloomington: Indiana University Press.

————. (1991). The Politics of Personal Knowledge. In C. Witherell and N. Noddings, eds., *Stories Lives Tell: Narrative and Dialogue in Education*, 67–77. New York: Teachers College Press.

————. (1988). *Bitter Milk: Women and Teaching*. Amherst: University of Massachusetts Press.

Hamilton, D. (1993). Texts, Literacy, and Schooling. In B. Green, ed., *The Insistence of the Letter: Literacy Studies and Curriculum Theorizing*, 46–57. Pittsburg: University of Pittsburg Press.

Harman, S. and Edelsky, C. (1989). The Risks of Whole Language: Alienation and Connection. *Language Arts* 66: 4, 392–406.

Hilton, M., ed. (1996). *Potent Fictions: Children's Literacy and the Challenge of Popular Culture*. London: Routledge.

Holme, B. (1979). *Bulfinch's Mythology: The Greek and Roman Fables Illustrated*. New York: Viking Press.

hooks, b. (1992). *Black Looks: Race and Representation*. Toronto: between the lines.

———. (1994). Eros, Eroticism, and the Pedagogical Process. In H.A. Giroux and P. McLaren, eds., *Between Borders: Pedagogy and the Politics of Cultural Studies*, 113–118. New York: Routledge.

———. (1995, March-April). In Praise of Student/Teacher Romances: Notes on the Subversive Power of Passion. *UTNE Reader* 68, 37–8.

———. (1993). *Sisters of the Yam: Black Women and Self—Discovery*. Toronto: between the lines.

Horsman, J. (1990). *Something in My Mind Besides the Everyday*. Toronto: The Women's Press.

Jay, G. (1995). Taking Multiculturalism Personally: Ethnos and Ethos in the Classroom. In J. Gallop, ed., *Pedagogy: The Question of Impersonation*, 117–128. Bloomington: Indiana University Press.

Johnson, C. (1995). Disinfecting Dialogues. In J. Gallop, ed., *Pedagogy: The Question of Impersonation*, 129–137. Bloomington: Indiana University Press.

Johnson, R. (1983). What Is Cultural Studies Anyway? *Anglistica* 26: 1–2, 1–75.

Joyrich, L. (1995). Give Me a Girl at an Impressionable Age and She Is Mine for Life: Jean Brodie as Pedagogical Primer. In J. Gallop, ed., *Pedagogy: The Question of Impersonation*, 46–63. Bloomington: Indiana University Press.

Kaplan, A. (1993). *French Lessons: A Memoir*. Chicago: University of Chicago Press.

Kelly, U. (1993). *Marketing Place: Cultural Politics, Regionalism, and Reading*. Halifax: Fernwood Books.

Kincaid, J. (1988). *A Small Place*. London: Virago Press.

Lankshear, C. (1993). Curriculum as Literacy: Reading and Writing in "New Times." In B. Green, ed., *The Insistence of the Letter: Literacy Studies and Curriculum Theorizing*, 154–174. Pittsburg: University of Pittsburg.

———, and McLaren, P. (1993). Introduction. In C. Lankshear and P. McLaren, eds., *Critical Literacy: Politics, Praxis and the Postmodern Turn*, 1–56. Albany: SUNY Press.

Lather, P. (1991). *Getting Smart: Feminist Research and Pedagogy with/in the Postmodern*. New York: Routledge.

Lesko, N. (1988). The Curriculum of the Body: Lessons from a Catholic High School. In L.G. Roman, L.K. Christian-Smith, and E. Ellsworth, eds., *Becoming Feminine: The Politics of Popular Culture*, 123–142. New York: Falmer Press.

Lewis, M. (1993). *Without a Word: Teaching Beyond Women's Silence*. New York: Routledge.

Luke, A. (1991). Literacies as Social Practices. *English Education* 3: 3, 131–147.

———. (1991a). The Political Economy of Reading Instruction. In C.D. Baker and A. Luke, eds., *Towards a Sociology of Reading Pedagogy*, 3–25. Philadelphia: John Benjamins.

———. (1993). Series Editor's Introduction. In L.K. Christian-Smith, ed.,

Texts of Desire: Essays on Fiction, Femininity, and Schooling, vii–xiv. London: Falmer Press.

———. (1993a). Stories of Social Regulation: The Micropolitics of Classroom Narrative. In B. Green, ed., *The Insistence of the Letter: Literacy Studies and Curriculum Theorizing*, 137–153. Pittsburg: University of Pittsburg Press.

———. (1994). On Reading and the Sexual Division of Labour. *Journal of Curriculum Studies* 26: 4, 361–381.

Luke, C. (1993). Television Curriculum and Popular Literacy: Feminine Identity Politics and Family Discourse. In B. Green, ed., *The Insistence of the Letter: Literacy Studies and Curriculum Theorizing*, 175–194. Pittsburg: University of Pittsburgh Press.

———, and Bishop, G. (1994). Selling and Reading Gender and Culture. *The Australian Journal of Language and Literacy* 17: 2, 109–119.

———, and Gore, J. (1992). Women in the Academy: Strategy, Struggle, Survival. In C. Luke and J. Gore, eds., *Feminisms and Critical Pedagogy*, 192–210. New York: Routledge.

Macedo, D. (1993). Literacy for Stupification: The Pedagogy of Big Lies. *Harvard Educational Review* 63: 2, 183–206.

Mamer, K. (1995). Untitled. *trip*, 1.

Martusewicz, R.A. (1992). Mapping the Terrain of the Post-Modern Subject: Post-Structuralism and the Educated Woman. In W.F. Pinar and W.M. Reynolds, eds., *Understanding Curriculum as Phenomenological and Deconstructed Text*, 131–158. New York: Teachers College Press.

Matheison, M. (1975). *The Preachers of Culture*. London: Allen & Unwin.

McLaren, P. (1995). *Critical Pedagogy and Predatory Culture*. New York: Routledge.

———. (1994). *Life in Schools* (2nd ed.). New York: Longman.

———. (1994a). Multiculturalism and the Post-Modern Critique: Toward a Pedagogy of Resistance and Transformation. In H.A. Giroux and P. McLaren, eds., *Between Borders: Pedagogy and the Politics of Cultural Studies*, 192–222. New York: Routledge.

———, and Hammer, R. (1992). Media Knowledge, Warrior Citizenry, and Postmodern Literacies. *Journal of Curriculum Theorizing* 10: 2, 29–68.

McRobbie, A. (1994). *Postmodernism and Popular Culture*. New York: Routledge.

Miller, N. (1991). *Getting Personal: Autobiography as Cultural Criticism*. New York: Routledge.

Mohanty, C.T. (1994). On Race and Voice: Challenges for Liberal Education in the 1990's. In H.A. Giroux and P. McLaren, eds., *Between Borders: Pedagogy and the Politics of Cultural Studies*, 145–166. New York: Routledge.

Moi, T. (1985). *Sexual/Textual Politics*. New York: Methuen.

Morford, M.P.O. and Lenardon, R.J. (1977). *Classical Mythology* (2nd ed.). New York: Longman.

Morgan, B. (1987). Three Dreams of Language: Or, No Longer Immured in the Bastille of the Humanist Word. *College English* 49: 4, 449–458.

Morgan, R. (1990). The "Englishness" of English Teaching. In I. Goodson and P. Medway, eds., *Bringing English to Order,* 197–241. London: Falmer Press.

———. (1993). Transitions from English to Cultural Studies. *Curriculum and Teaching* 8: 1, 103–129.

———. (1995). Three Unspeakable Things: Looking Through English's Family Album. *The Journal of Educational Thought* 29: 1, 3–33.

Morley, D. and Chen, K., eds. (1996). *Stuart Hall: Critical Dialogues in Cultural Studies.* New York: Routledge.

Morris, M. (1993). Things to do with Shopping Malls. In S. During, ed., *Cultural Studies Reader,* 295–319. New York: Routledge.

Moss, G. (1993). The Place for Romance in Young People's Writing. In L.K. Christian-Smith, ed., *Texts of Desire: Essays on Fiction, Femininity, and Schooling,* 106–125. London: Falmer Press.

———. (1989). *Un/Popular Fictions.* London: Virago.

Munro, A. (1971). *Lives of Girls and Women.* Toronto: McGraw-Hill Ryerson.

Munt, S.R. (1994). *Murder by the Book: Feminism and the Crime Novel.* New York: Routledge.

Noddings, N. and Witherell, C., eds. (1991). *Stories Lives Tell: Narrative and Dialogue in Education.* New York: Teachers College Press.

Ogbu, J.U. (1983). Literacy and Schooling in Subordinate Cultures: The Case of Black Americans. In D.P. Resnick, ed., *Literacy in Historical Perspective,* 129–153. Washington: Library of Congress.

Pagano, J. (1990). *Exiles and Communities: Teaching in the Patriarchal Wilderness.* Albany: SUNY Press.

———. (1991). Moral Fictions: The Dilemma of Theory and Practice. In C. Witherall and N. Noddings, eds., *Stories Lives Tell: Narrative and Dialogue in Education,* 193–206. New York: Teachers College Press.

———. (1994). Teaching Women. In L. Stone, ed., *The Education Feminism Reader,* 252–275. New York: Routledge.

Patterson, A. (1992). Individualism in English: From Personal Growth to Discursive Construction. *English Education* 24: 3, 131–146.

Pinar, W.F. and Reynolds, W.M.(1992). Genealogical Notes: The History of Phenomenology and Post-Structuralism in Curriculum Studies. In W.F. Pinar and W.M. Reynolds, eds., *Understanding Curriculum as Phenomenological and Deconstructed Text,* 237–261. New York: Teachers College Press.

Portelli, J. (1995). Reconsidering Whole Language: A Critical/Philosophical Perspective. *The English Quarterly* 27: 1–2, 7–9.

Postrel, V. and Gillespie, N. (1995, March-April). On Borders and Belonging: An Interview with Richard Rodriquez. *UTNE Reader* 68, 76–79.

Radway, J. (1986). *Reading the Romance: Women, Patriarchy, and Popular Literature.* Chapel Hill: University of North Carolina Press.

Rich, A. (1986). *Blood, Bread, and Poetry: Selected Prose 1979–1985.* New York: W.W. Norton.

Robinson, H.S. and Wilson, K. (1950). *The Encyclopaedia of Myths and Legends of All Nations*. London: Kaye & Ward, Ltd.

Rockhill, K. (1993). Dis/Connecting Literacy and Sexuality: Speaking the Unspeakable in the Classroom. In C. Lankshear and P. McLaren, eds., *Critical Literacy: Politics, Praxis, and the Postmodern*, 335–366. Albany: SUNY Press.

———. (1991). Literacy as Threat/Desire: Longing to be SOMEBODY. In J. Gaskell and A. McLaren, eds., *Women and Education* (2nd ed.), 333–349. Calgary: Detselig.

Rodriguez, R. (1982). *Hunger of Memory: The Education of Richard Rodriguez*. New York: Bantam Books.

Roman, L.G and Christian-Smith, L.K. (1988). Introduction. In L.G. Roman, L.K. Christian-Smith and E. Ellsworth, eds., *Becoming Feminine: The Politics of Popular Culture*, 1–34. New York: Falmer Press.

Said, E. (1989). Representing the Colonized: Anthropology's Interlocutors. *Critical Inquiry* 15, 205–225.

Scheman, N. (1995). On Waking Up One Morning and Discovering We Are Them. In J. Gallop, ed., *Pedagogy: The Question of Impersonation*, 106–116. Bloomington: Indiana University Press.

Schenke, A. (1991). The "Will to Reciprocity" and the Work of Memory: Fictioning Speaking out of Silence in E.S.L. and Feminist Pedagogy. *Resouces for Feminist Research* 20: 3/4, 47–55.

Scholle, D. and Denski, S. (1993). Reading and Writing the Media: Critical Media Literacy and Postmodernism. In C. Lankshear and P. McLaren, eds., *Critical Literacy: Politics, Praxis, and the Postmodern*, 297–321. Albany: SUNY Press.

Shields, C. (1993). *The Stone Diaries*. Toronto: Vintage Books.

Shumway, D.R. (1989). Reading Rock 'n' Roll in the Classroom: A Critical Pedagogy. In H.A. Giroux and P. McLaren, eds., *Critical Pedagogy, the State, and Cultural Struggle*, 222–235. Albany: SUNY Press.

Silverman, K. (1983). *The Subject of Semiotics*. Oxford: Oxford University Press.

———. (1996). *The Threshold of the Visible World*. New York: Routledge.

Simon, R. (1992). *Teaching Against the Grain: Texts for a Pedagogy of Possibility*. South Hadley: Bergin & Garvey.

Simon, R.I. (1995). Face to Face with Alterity: Postmodern Jewish Identity and the Eros of Pedagogy. In J. Gallop, ed., *Pedagogy: The Question of Impersonation*, 90–105. Bloomington: Indiana University Press.

Spencer, M. (1986). Emergent Literacies: A Site for Analysis. *Language Arts* 63: 5, 442–453.

Spivak, G.C. (1990). Questions of Multi-Culturalism. In S. Harasym, ed., *The Post-Colonial Critic: Interviews, Strategies, Dialogues*. New York: Routledge.

———. (1994). Strategies of Vigilance: An Interview with Gayatri Chakravorty Spivak. In A. McRobbie, *Postmodernism and Popular Culture*, 121–131. New York: Routledge.

Steedman, C.K. (1986). *Landscape for a Good Woman*. New Brunswick, NJ: Rutgers University Press.

Taubman, P. (1992). Achieving the Right Distance. In W.F. Pinar and W.M. Reynolds, eds., *Understanding Curriculum as Phenomenological and Deconstructed Text*, 216–233. New York: Teachers College Press.

Taylor, S. (1993). Transforming the Texts: Towards a Feminist Classroom Practice. In L.K. Christian-Smith, ed., *Texts of Desire: Essays on Fiction, Femininity, and Schooling*, 126–144. London: Falmer Press.

Tisch, S. and Finerman, W., producers, and Zemeckis, R., director. (1994). *Forrest Gump* [film]. Hollywood, CA: Paramount Pictures.

Walkerdine, V. (1990). *School Girl Fictions*. London: Verso.

Walcott, R. (1995). Hip Hop Puts Fashion to Work. *This Magazine* 28, 51–53.

West, C. (1993). The New Cultural Politics of Difference. In S. During, ed., *The Cultural Studies Reader*, 203–217. New York: Routledge.

———. (1993a). *Race Matters*. Boston: Beacon Press.

Whatley, M.H. (1988). Raging Hormones and Powerful Cars: The Construction of Men's Sexuality in School Sex Education Popular Adolescent Films. *Journal of Education* 170: 3, 100–121.

Williamson, J. (1981/2). How Does Girl Number Twenty Understand Ideology? *Screen Education*, 40, 80–87.

Willinsky, J. (1994). After 1492–1992: A Post-Colonial Supplement for the Canadian Curriculum. *Journal of Curriculum Studies* 26: 6, 613–629.

———. (1990). *The New Literacy: Redefining Reading and Writing in the Schools*. New York: Routledge.

———, and Hunniford, M. (1993). Reading the Romance Younger: The Mirrors and Fears of a Preparatory Literature. In L.K. Christian-Smith, ed., *Texts of Desire: Essays on Fiction, Femininity, and Schooling*, 87–105. London: Falmer Press.

Winterson, J. (1992). *Written on the Body*. London: Vintage.

Wright, E. (1984). *Psychoanalytic Criticism: Theory in Practice*. New York: Methuen.

■ Index